# Reader's Digest True LIVES

## stories of Hope, Honor & Humor

UNFORGETTABLE WRITING FROM
THE WORLD'S MOST POPULAR MAGAZINE

Reader's Digest

THE READER'S DIGEST ASSOCIATION, INC.
PLEASANTVILLE, NEW YORK • MONTREAL

# True Lives

| | |
|---|---|
| Vice President, Development | Frank Lalli |
| Editor | Steve Gelman |
| Managing Editor | Kathleen Baxter |
| Design | Priest Media, Inc. |
| Cover Design | Michele Laseau |
| Production Associate | Erick Swindell |
| Rights & Permissions | Sandy McCormick Hill |

**Reader's Digest Books**

| | |
|---|---|
| Editor in Chief | Neil Wertheimer |
| Managing Editor | Suzanne G. Beason |
| Art Director | Michele Laseau |
| Production Technology Director | Doug Croll |
| Manufacturing Manager | John L. Cassidy |
| President and Publisher, Trade Publishing | Harold Clarke |
| President, U.S. Books & Home Entertainment | Dawn Zier |

**Reader's Digest Association, Inc.**

| | |
|---|---|
| President, North America Global Editor in Chief | Eric Schrier |

Library of Congress Cataloging-in-Publication Data

True Lives : Stories of Hope, Honor, and Humor : The Best Stories from 83 Years of Reader's Digest.
    p. cm.

  ISBN: 0-7621-0741-3 (hdcvr)
 1.  Biography--20th century. 2.  Inspiration. 3.  United States--Biography.  I. Reader's Digest Association.
  CT120.T78 2006
  920.009'04--dc22

                         2005029274

Address any comments about *True Lives* to:
The Reader's Digest Association, Inc.
Editor-in-Chief, Books and Music Reader's Digest Road
Pleasantville, NY 10570-7000

To order copies of *True Lives*, call 1-800-846-2100.

Visit our website at **rd.com**

Printed in the United States of America
1  3  5  7  9  10  8  6  4  2

# Introduction

Most people think the key to great writing is a mastery of words. This makes for a wonderful stereotype—the solitary writer sitting in front of his typewriter, fingers dancing like a pianist's, tattered thesaurus by his side, hours passing by unnoticed, emotions surging with the good sentences and plunging with every press of the "delete" key. You can just see the mountain of crumpled paper surrounding the trash can, can't you?

It is a romantic Hollywood vision of writing, which of course means it is utterly false. Great writing doesn't happen at the keyboard. It happens long before the writer sits down to type.

In journalism school, would-be writers are taught that 90 percent of their job is research; a great story, once the facts are gathered, practically writes itself. You'd be surprised at how many newspaper articles are researched for days and then written in an hour. Magazine writers, book authors, even speechwriters know that this holds true for them as well. This is the dirty little secret of the writing profession—the hardest work is in the observation.

The writers in *True Lives* are all gifted wordsmiths, but where they excel most is in their ability to observe the details of the world around them. By seeking out interesting people, asking the right questions, being at the right place, and listening with undivided attention, they accumulate stories so rich in detail that when they are finally ready to write, the words are mostly there.

For more than 80 years, *Reader's Digest* magazine has provided its readers with stories about heroes and villains, the famous and the obscure, the mundane and the magnificent. Other magazines are known for being more "literary." But for honest, effective storytelling, we take pride in the fact that *Reader's Digest* is the place the world turns to, month in and month out, year in and year out. Today, *Reader's Digest* is published in some 50 editions in 20 languages, reaching an estimated 80 million readers a month. It is without question the world's most widely read magazine. And for one simple reason: It is filled with great stories.

In looking back over the first 1,000 issues of *Reader's Digest* magazine in search of the best of the best, we quickly discovered this was an impossible task. At *Reader's Digest*, the goal has always been to make the writer transparent to the reader. Rather than relying on stylish writing, we pursue simple language, crisp sentences and clear description. The result is that the people in the stories get the focus, not the writer. And so, in selecting the stories for this book, we quickly realized it wasn't about which stories had the most flawless sentences, but rather which people and tales were the most interesting and timeless.

Many of the authors in this unique collection are famous, either as professional writers or as masters of their fields. Margaret Mead, Albert Schweitzer and Ronald Reagan are good examples of the latter—people who reached the very top of their fields, yet still had the perspective to report on what they learned with humility and simplicity. There are many famous authors here as well, such as James Michener and Carl Sandburg, whose writing gifts require no introduction and who are undisputed masters of the simple direct sentence.

But it's not the authors who are the stars of *True Lives* but rather the people they are writing about. From U.S. Presidents to battle-scarred soldiers, impoverished children to beloved entertainers, the cast of characters in *True Lives* run the gamut of life experiences. What links them all is their ability to rise up and excel even in the most challenging of circumstances. As you read their stories, we hope the words engage you. But much more so, we hope the people who inspired these stories will lift your hearts and give you hope.

Neil Wertheimer
Editor-in-Chief
Reader's Digest Books

# Table of Contents

# Amy's Choice

Amy Waldroop's daily world was a disaster. Her mother was a junkie, Amy was flunking out of school and her siblings were ill fed and ill treated. Amy knew she had to do something to save her family.

*By Rena Dictor LeBlanc*

~

It was nearly midnight by the time 19-year-old Amy Waldroop returned to her cramped apartment in Orange, Calif., and she was exhausted. After a full day's work at a florist shop, she had put in another six hours waitressing before heading home.

Pushing the key into the lock, she quietly opened the door so as not to wake her younger siblings. She stepped into the front room—and froze. The apartment was in shambles: plates of half-eaten food were scattered in front of the TV; toys littered the floor; clothes, shoes and homework were strewn everywhere. Amy's eyes welled with tears.

This is just way too much for me, she thought. Her worst fears began racing through her mind, and soon she was sobbing. Would

ILLUSTRATION BY PETER KNOCK

the court tell her she couldn't care for her family anymore? Would the kids go through the torture once more of being split up and sent away? She was so young, almost a child herself, and yet Amy knew everything depended on her. Everything. At that moment, she wondered if she would ever find the strength to see it through.

**Amy Waldroop had been born dead.** Physicians fought and saved this smaller twin of a drug-addicted mother, and she'd had to fight for everything in life ever since.

From earliest childhood, Amy took care of her younger siblings. First, it was her sister Amanda, four years younger. Then, when Amy was 10, along came Adam, followed by Joseph and finally Anthony. With a mother so often wasted—if not gone altogether—it frequently fell to Amy to feed and diaper the babies, lull them to sleep when they cried and care for them when they were sick.

Once, when the children all came down with chicken-pox, Amy wound up at the drugstore asking the clerk what to do. Handed some calamine, the 10-year-old stared at the instructions on the bottle, unable to make sense of

# Amy and her twin went without meals because their mother didn't sign them up for a free lunch. They would sit hungry in the schoolyard and watch the other kids gobble sandwiches.

them. Back home she bundled her siblings into the shower and afterward spread the lotion on them with bunched up toilet paper. They healed.

Jan, their mother, only added to the family chaos by careering in and out of her children's lives. Sometimes they lived in apartments, sometimes in shelters or drug-infested motels.

At school—when the kids attended—they kept mostly to themselves, not wanting classmates to know how they

were living. But it inevitably showed. Amy and her twin, Jessica, for instance, went without meals there because Jan sometimes failed to sign them up for the lunch programs. They would sit hungry and desolate in the schoolyard as the other kids gobbled their sandwiches.

Meals at home were a different challenge: When Jan was around, the twins were expected to cook. Once, a boyfriend of Jan's became enraged because Amy did not have dinner promptly on the table. He grabbed the child by the hair and threw her against the refrigerator.

The girl suffered other violence and finally told her social worker. The woman was stunned. "My God, why didn't you tell me before?" she asked. "I thought we'd be taken away," Amy replied.

Two weeks later social workers came knocking, and the young girl's nightmare unfolded. Amy and Jessica were to be taken to a juvenile detention center. Meanwhile, Amy watched, distraught, as her other siblings were trundled out to waiting cars, bound for separate foster homes. Looking into their anguished faces, she could only manage to say, "I'm so sorry. I'm so sorry."

The kids, lonely and depressed, spent six months apart from one another until they were sent to live with their maternal grandmother. Although Jan was forbidden to stay with her children, Amy's grandmother took pity on her daughter and allowed her to re-enter the children's lives, plunging them back into chaos. At 14, Jessica left home for good.

Meanwhile, all the children were falling further and further behind in school. As a ninth-grader, Amy could read only at a fourth-grade level. With envy she studied the kids who dressed well and excelled in class, and she wished she could somehow enter their world. And leave hers behind forever.

**Walking across the school grounds one day,** Amy spotted a table littered with college brochures. She browsed through pictures of spacious campuses and happy, contented kids—all of it looking impossibly glamorous and unachievable.

But a guidance counselor soon gave her unexpected hope. Amy could attend college, she was told, and for free. It would take a scholarship, though, and for that she'd need much better grades. Amy immediately signed up for summer school.

During her junior and senior years, she diligently attended classes, then went to work after school from 3:30 to 11:30, returned to her grandmother's place and plowed through homework till the early hours of the morning.

Amy's resolve was strengthened further during these tough months by a boy she met at school, Jerry Robinson.* For the first time in her life, Amy felt that someone really listened to her and truly cared. Their friendship turned to love, and Amy had no doubt that the two would marry and have children together.

But during this time, unbeknown to the social workers, Jan had come to live in her mother's house, throwing the family into fresh tumult. Amy's grandmother couldn't turn her daughter out of her home, even when Jan was high on drugs. One afternoon Amy was summoned to Villa Park High School. A social worker was waiting for her.

"We know your mother has been staying with you," the social worker said, "and that Joey pricked his finger on a drug needle." Amy braced herself, knowing what was coming next. "We're going to have to put you guys in foster care."

"No! Don't split us up!" the girl blurted. "Can't you just leave it the way it is?"

The social worker shook his head. Amy's voice then rose like the howl of a lioness protecting her cubs: "Why can't I take care of them? I take care of them all the time anyway."

The social worker hesitated, then said, "Maybe. Once you're 18, you could apply to become their relative caretaker. Then you'd be their foster mother until we find a home where all of you can be together."

"I'll do it," Amy said. She hadn't a clue what was involved, but that mattered little. She would just forge ahead, a day at a time, as she had all her life. And, somehow, she would make things turn out.

**Amy soon realized the full price of her commitment.** One afternoon she came walking home from school, clutching a sheet of paper. It was a letter from U.C.L.A., inviting her to come see the lush campus. It was what she'd longed for, a place where no one would know about her awful background, where she could study to become someone special—a nurse, perhaps, or maybe even an attorney.

Yet the letter only ripped Amy apart inside. The entire walk home she kept imagining herself at this prestigious university, kept picturing a life free of the worries and duties she'd always known.

Then, as she turned a corner, she saw her brothers playing outside her grandmother's house, running, laughing. Adam. Joey. Tony. She'd diapered and fed them, read them stories, sung them songs. Her dreams for herself, she realized, were no match for the love

etched in her soul. She crumpled the letter up and threw it away.

**One month later, after tediously filing piles of paperwork,** Amy sat before a judge in family court. "You're so young," the judge said to her. "Are you sure you want this responsibility?"

"There's no other way to keep my family together," Amy replied simply. The judge's ultimate decision was a remarkable victory for an 18-year-old girl: Amy was named guardian of her siblings for a six-month trial period.

> "Guys, all that we have is each other. If you want to stay together, we've got to show we're responsible. And you need to watch your tongues."

Meanwhile, instead of going to her high school prom, Amy had searched for a place to live. Finally she found a run-down one-bedroom unit. The salary from her two jobs—as a florist-shop clerk and as a waitress—along with her savings and foster-care payments from the state of California enabled her to pay the first and last months' rent.

Her siblings didn't make her task any easier in the months ahead. The boys sometimes ditched school and would curse at Amy when they were angry. And she had more than a few face-offs with Amanda.

"You're not my mom!" the 14-year-old would shout at Amy when things grew particularly tense.

One day Adam rebelled at doing his reading assignment for school, hurling his book across the room. Only after some coaxing did he tell Amy what was really going on.

"Every kid in the class can read," Adam said, bursting into tears, "and I can't."

Remembering her own shame about reading, Amy began taking all the kids to the library. And for many weeks afterward she set aside special time to tutor each of

---

*Name has been changed to protect privacy.*

them separately. Adam took pride in the way his reading skills improved.

As always, though, a fresh obstacle appeared—one that came as a huge shock to Amy. Despite taking birth control pills, she became pregnant with Jerry's child. The timing was horrible, but there was no way she'd consider either abortion or giving up the baby. Her love would enfold this child just as it had the others. And so another little boy, Donavin, entered Amy's life at age 19.

The strain of things built up remorselessly. Finally it reached a breaking point that late night when Amy returned from work to an apartment in shambles. She had left the boys in the care of Amanda, who had fallen asleep in Amy's bed.

Shaken, Amy felt overwhelmed once more by the enormousness of all she had taken on. But she knew she had no choice: She could never let her siblings be ripped away from one another again. To make it as a family, she'd just have to get them to work together.

"All of you, get in here right now!" she yelled, trembling with frustration.

The three boys stumbled into the room. "How could you do this?" she asked, her words coming in a torrent. "You know they're checking up on us."

Within a few minutes, the wave of anger ebbed. "Guys," she said more gently, "all that we have is each other. If you want to stay together past six months, we've got to show we're responsible. We've got to keep this place neat.

"And you need to watch your tongues. Also, don't eat all the food as soon as I buy it, or there won't be any next week. And you have to be bleeding before you can miss school." Startled, the kids agreed to begin pulling their weight.

Unfortunately, Jerry soon asked that Amy choose between a life with him and their child or continuing to care for her siblings. She chose—and the relationship ended.

If anything, Amy grew more tenacious with every setback. And her efforts were rewarded when the court allowed her to continue as guardian.

To the boys, this was an enormous comfort. But Amy's relationship with her younger sister continued to sour. At 15, Amanda finally went to live with an aunt.

Now left with Donavin and the three boys, Amy dangled a prize before them: "If we save enough for a deposit, we'll get a house of our own," she said. "And we'll even get a dog." Nothing could have been more tantalizing to them.

**Amy's relief at remaining the kids' guardian** was undermined by the pressure she always felt to measure up. The boys were still dependents of the court. Social workers still looked regularly over her shoulder and asked the boys humiliating questions: "Does she feed you? Does she ever try to harm you?" There was no way she could be sure her siblings would never be taken away again.

Or so she assumed, until the day a visiting social worker dropped a bombshell. "We'd like to get the boys out of foster care and adopted into homes," she said. Sensing that the family was about to be split apart yet again, Amy replied, "Fine, then. Call it adoption if you want, but they're not going anywhere." To Amy's surprise, the social worker took her terse remark seriously. She explained that if Amy were to adopt the boys, they would become like any other family. They'd be free to live their lives without constant monitoring.

That night at dinner Amy told the boys about the idea. "Cool!" Joey said. And with playful exuberance he threw a piece of corn at Adam. His brother flicked it back, and pretty soon corn was flying.

Amy rolled her eyes. They didn't have far to go to be like any other family.

Once she began struggling with the rules and paperwork for adoption, Amy felt intimidated and often lost. At last, in a hearing in March 1999, the family appeared before Judge Gail Andler, who terminated the parental rights of Jan and the father of Anthony. This was a major step toward full adoption. The judge's eyes filled as she addressed Amy. "I'm very proud of you," she said. "Not many family members would do what you're doing, especially for this many children."

Judge Andler then turned to the three boys. "The next time I see you, you'll be heading for adoption. How do you feel about that?"

"And we won't ever have to leave the family?" Joey asked.

The judge shook her head. "The plan is for you to be a family forever."

The final step came this past November. Amy's siblings sat on either side of her in Judge Andler's court as the young woman signed three separate papers—one for each of the boys. As the proceedings ended, Amy thanked everyone. "No," Judge Andler responded, "thank you. You saved three kids."

**On a lazy spring day, in a modest Anaheim neighborhood,** Amy stood in front of a neatly kept one-story house. She watched her brothers playing basketball and heard the playful bark of their dog, Tahoe. The young woman had made good on her promise: They had rented a home, a real home, and the boys had gotten their dog. Above all, Amy relished knowing that her family was now a world away from the mean streets they had once known. As if on cue, she heard the tinkling of music of an approaching ice-cream truck. And, like any mother, she went to round up her kids.

**Amy continues to raise her family alone,** but has begun taking courses in business management at a nearby community college. Eventually, she hopes to become a child psychologist. ∎

# LIFE IN THESE UNITED STATES

**WHEN I BOUGHT** my new Lexus Sport Coupe, my two sons asked me who would inherit it if I met my demise. I pondered the question, then told them if I passed away on an even day, the son born on an even day would get it. If it happened on an odd day, the one born on an odd day would get it.

A few weekends later, while river rafting with one of my sons, I was tossed out of the boat. As I floated in the rapids, I heard my son yelling, "It's the wrong day!"

-GREG ZARET, MISSION VIEJO, CALIF.

**WITH A NEW BOOK** on handwriting analysis, I began practicing on colleagues at work. One skeptical woman asked if she could bring in a sample of her daughter's writing. "Of course," I replied.

The next day the woman handed me an envelope. I opened it, read the contents, then dramatically told her, "Your daughter is 14 years old. She's an A student. She loves music and horses."

Amazed, the woman ran off to tell her friends before I could show her the note. It read, "I'm 14 years old and an A student. I love music and horses. My mother thinks you're a fake."

-BILL WHITMAN, WEST HILLS, CALIF.

**MY MOTHER** is always trying to understand what motivates people, especially those in her family. One day she and my sister were talking about one relative's bad luck. "Why do you suppose she changed jobs?" she asked my sister. "Maybe she has a subconscious desire not to succeed."

"Or maybe it just happened," said my sister, exasperated. "Do you know you analyze everything to death?"

Mother was silent for a moment. "That's true," she said. "Why do you think I do that?"

-BOBBIE S. CYPHERS, HOT SPRINGS, N.C.

**I'M A STICKLER** about people spelling my first name correctly: K-A-T-H-Y. One day I went to an electronics store where they ask for your name when you buy something. I told the clerk my name is Kathy with a K. He didn't say anything as I paid for my goods and left the store. Later when I looked at my receipt, I saw that he had noted my name: Cathy Withakay.

-KATHY LANDERKIN, BALTIMORE, MD.

**THERE WAS A TIME** when I wore a wig to work. It was convenient and, I thought, matched my real hair perfectly. One day I was on the elevator when a woman got on. Staring at my head, she said, "If you don't mind my asking, is that a wig?"

"Why, yes," I said.

"Wow," she replied. "You'd never know it."

-EMMA M. LEE, PHILADELPHIA, PA.

**I WAS IN** a department store when I heard on the public-address system that the optical department was offering free ice cream. I headed down the escalator to take advantage of the offer, trying to decide on vanilla or chocolate. I was nearly drooling when I got to the optical section and said to the clerk, "I'm here for my ice cream."

"Ice cream?" came the reply. "Sorry. What we have is a free eye screening."

-ROSANNE L. BARNETT, ALPHARETTA, GA.

**AFTER BOOKING** my 90-year-old mother on a flight from Florida to Nevada, I called the airline to go over her needs. The woman representative listened patiently as I requested a wheelchair and an attendant for my mother because of her arthritis and impaired vision. I also asked for a special meal and assistance in changing planes.

My apprehension lightened a bit when the woman assured me everything would be taken care of. I thanked her profusely.

"Why, you're welcome," she replied. I was about to hang up when she cheerfully asked, "And will your mother be needing a rental car?"

-THOMAS CORBETT, LAS VEGAS, NEV.

**ONE DAY** my housework-challenged husband decided to wash his sweatshirt. Seconds after he stepped into the laundry room, he shouted to me, "What setting do I use on the washing machine?"

"It depends," I replied. "What does it say on your shirt?"

"University of Oklahoma," he yelled back.

-JERRI BOYER, PONCA CITY, OKLA.

# The Secret

*By Richard Reeves*

The man entrusted with the fate of nations needed steroids, amphetamines, painkillers and other pills to keep going day after day.

# Pain of JFK

n September 21, 1947, a 30-year-old American Congressman collapsed in Claridge's, the London hotel, and a friend got him to a clinic. Luckily for him, the friend, Pamela Digby Churchill, had been the daughter-in-law of Winston Churchill and was a woman well connected enough to send one of London's most prominent physicians, Daniel Davies, to the young man's bedside. After an examination, the doctor told Pam Churchill, "That young American friend of yours—he hasn't a year to live."

The Congressman was John F. Kennedy. He had heard words like that most of his life. He had already been given the last rites of the Roman Catholic Church at least twice as a young man. He always expected to die young, and because

As a child, John F. Kennedy spent months in bed with a range of illnesses, beginning with a severe bout of scarlet fever, which put him into the hospital for two months before his third birthday. Growing up, he read most of the time, racing through books of history and heroism, as healthier kids played outside. "Life is unfair," he said famously. Some are born sick, and some are born well. Some are born rich, and some are born poor.

He was born sick, and he developed a fatalism and a sense of the irony of life that was his true ideology. "They were mentally measuring me for a coffin," he wrote to a buddy as a teenager during one of his long hospital stays. He had great personal courage in dealing with almost constant pain. He also lied and cheated to get what he wanted before it was too late for him. The boy reading of war became a young man determined to share in the great experience of his generation, World War II. He could never have passed a real military physical examination, so he used the riches and influence of his father, Joseph P. Kennedy, to become a naval officer. The old man persuaded friends in the military to accept a certificate of good health, a false one, from a family doctor.

In the South Pacific, after a Japanese destroyer ran down his boat, PT 109, Lieutenant Kennedy was strong enough and courageous enough to swim for hours, pulling along one of his men, wounded and badly burned, by holding on to the strap of the man's life jacket in his teeth. His executive officer, Leonard Thom, wrote home that Kennedy was the only man in the Navy who faked good health. After the war, Kennedy survived as something of a medical miracle, kept alive and walking with complicated combinations of injections and pills, some of them pretty dangerous stuff, along with regular hospital stays.

of that, he lived life as a race, running against his own mortality.

Boy and man, Jack Kennedy ran and ran against the clock. He took everything he could get as fast as he could get it, refusing to wait his turn. Rules were for others, for the people who had more time than he did. JFK, as he came to be known, figured out a way to get around the leaders of his party and became, at 43, the youngest man ever elected President. He looked like a god, and few people knew or suspected that the man entrusted with the fate of nations was always accompanied by doctors and aides carrying an array of steroids, amphetamines, painkillers and other pills and potions that kept him alive and going day after day.

Most of the people he met as President had not a clue that he was a sick man. And he was not about to tell them. If anyone asked, he lied. And laughed. And he kept on laughing. Kennedy loved a little proverb he thought was

Irish, but actually came from the Indian epic *Ramayana*. "There are three things which are real: God, human folly and laughter. The first two are beyond our comprehension, so we must do what we can with the third."

On the day young Kennedy collapsed in London, Davies discovered that his emergency patient had the fatal affliction called Addison's disease, an autoimmune destruction of the adrenal glands resulting in low blood pressure, low energy levels and increased complications from infection. American doctors were soon to discover that cortisone injections would extend the short life spans of Addison's sufferers. Kennedy's wealthy father placed corticosteroids in safe-deposit boxes around the world—and the son was forever dependent on daily shots and drugs, along with time-release implants of the medication. As President, Kennedy was accompanied by two aides carrying "black bags": one of the bags contained the codes and procedures for launching nuclear attacks; the other was filled with the pharmaceuticals he needed every day to stay alive.

That was, as scholars and researchers have learned over the years, only part of it. The always tanned and brown-haired Kennedy—bronzed skin and hair color are Addison's symptoms—suffered from a range of maladies that would fill pages of any medical text. He was hospitalized or received regular treatment for recurring stomach and colon problems, a range of mysterious allergies, some hearing loss in one ear and a chronic venereal disease he contracted as a teenager. His low resistance to infection produced fevers as high as 105 degrees. That happened at least once during his years in the White House.

**In October of 1954, racked by debilitating back pain,** Kennedy, who had been elected to the U.S. Senate in 1952, was scheduled for an operation at the New York Hospital for Special Surgery. His office issued statements that produced matter-of-fact stories with lines like "to clear up a wartime injury" and "suffered a spinal injury in action in the Solomon Islands."

Those were lies. The truth was that he was risking his life to try to end the back problems that had plagued him since childhood. Even after doctors told him there was only a 50-50 chance that he would survive the surgery—Addison's episodes can be triggered by trauma—he went ahead. "This is the one that kills you or cures you," he told a couple of trusted assistants. To a hospital doctor he said, "I'd rather be dead than spend the rest of my life on these goddamned crutches."

He did survive the fusion of his deteriorating spinal vertebrae. But the lengthy operation was not a success.

Multiple infections kept him bedridden for weeks; he was unable to return to Washington for more than six months. Politicians and journalists, a lot less aggressive than they are now, knew Kennedy had been hospitalized, but they did not delve into his medical history.

Katharine Graham, whose husband Philip was publisher of the Washington *Post* and a close friend of Kennedy's, told me that after 50 years she still vividly remembered tears welling up as she watched young Jack Kennedy on crutches, slowly climbing up a steep stairway from a beach on Martha's Vineyard. Ten years later, he was running for President. It was his brother Robert's job to tell *Today's Health* magazine that JFK was in "superb physical condition."

"Tell them I don't have Addison's disease," JFK ordered during the general election campaign against Vice

> # Kennedy had great courage in dealing with almost constant pain. He also lied and cheated to get what he wanted before it was too late for him.

President Richard Nixon when Pierre Salinger, his press secretary, told him reporters were asking pointed questions, based on rumors. "They're saying you're taking cortisone," said Salinger.

"Well, I used to take cortisone, but I don't take it anymore."

In fact, he was taking it regularly. An old Navy buddy, Paul Fay, watched Kennedy injecting himself in the thigh and said, "Jack, the way you take that jab, it looks like it doesn't even hurt."

Kennedy lunged at him, stabbing him in the leg. Fay screamed in pain.

"It feels the same way to me," said Kennedy.

**Once inside the Oval Office, the President,** whose brother Bobby believed he suffered pain every day of his life, continued to take anything he could get his hands on. He was far more promiscuous with pharmaceuticals than he ever was with women. In late 1961, Bobby discovered that Jack was taking amphetamines, administered by Dr. Max Jacobson, who would later become infamous as "Dr. Feelgood," a New York doctor dispensing speed to a list of celebrities and socialites. When Bobby confronted his brother about Jacobson, JFK told him to mind his own business: "I don't care if it's horse piss. It works."

Jacobson was always on call for the White House. He would be summoned at any hour by a call saying he was needed by "Mrs. Dunn." The press knew none of this, publishing story after story and photo after photo about Kennedy's sailing and touch football on Cape Cod.

As far as the historical importance of Dr. Jacobson's amphetamine cocktails, we do know that Jacobson traveled to Vienna with Kennedy when JFK met there with Soviet Premier Khrushchev in June of 1961. Our leader came off second-best in his first negotiation with the Communist boss.

Whatever shape he was actually in, JFK was a cautious leader who almost always chose the more moderate options when war and peace were on the line. His finger was on the nuclear trigger during the Cuban Missile Crisis in October of 1962 and during a series of Berlin crises—and he neither pulled nor flinched. Most of the world considered him an effective and inspiring President with a gift for bringing out the best in people. They never knew the agonies of the dashing American leader. But some on his staff knew the truth. Kennedy conducted much of his business in bedside meetings, in bathrooms as he soaked in hot water or around the White House pool, which was heated to 87 degrees.

**At the White House in 1961,** Kennedy was confronted by the official White House physician, Adm. George Burkley, and a noted orthopedic surgeon, an Austrian immigrant named Hans Kraus, who was overseeing Kennedy's physical therapy. They called in Dr. Janet Travell, who by then was giving the President six or seven injections each day of procaine, a local anesthetic. The injections were extremely painful—his wife, Jacqueline, once heard him screaming in pain—but Kennedy craved the two hours of relief that came after each shot.

Burkley was worried that the President would soon be addicted to opiates or other painkillers. Kraus told him he would be a cripple before he ran for a second term. The Secret Service was already going over the original plans for the ramps Franklin D. Roosevelt had used to navigate the White House in a wheelchair.

"I will not treat this patient if she touches him again," said Kraus, a feisty little Austrian who had once ministered to his country's Olympic team. The President nodded. Burkley turned to Travell and said, "You understand? You keep your hands off the President!"

Under Kraus's supervision, Kennedy began exercising as many as five days a week in a small White House gym set up by Burkley. He did begin feeling better and was cutting back on painkillers. He may have been in the best shape of his adult life when he was murdered in Dallas on November 22, 1963, at the age of 46.

But he had won his race against death. Unwilling to wait his turn, he made his own rules and became the first self-selected President. Until his personal campaigning in almost every state in 1959 and early 1960, candidates of

> He did begin feeling better. He may have been in the best shape of his adult life when he was murdered in Dallas on November 22, at the age of 46.

both the Democratic and Republican parties were essentially selected by a party leadership of state and local chairmen ("bosses") in a convention every four years. Senator Kennedy hit the road, spending family money, mastering a newly dominant medium called television and setting up personal organizations in dozens of states. By the time Democratic leaders convened in Los Angeles—with older candidates like Adlai Stevenson, Senator Lyndon Johnson of Texas and Senator Stuart Symington of Missouri considered more formidable—Kennedy had almost enough delegates to win the nomination.

"That young man!" said a bitter Stevenson, who had been the party's nominee in 1952 and 1956. "He never says 'please,' and he never says 'I'm sorry.'"

Exactly right. JFK did not have the time for pleasantries. He did not know how long his tortured body would hold out. Looking back now, Kennedy can be seen as the icon of new generations who refused to wait for whatever they

wanted. He did not wait his turn. Now no one wants to. He had shown that the most important qualification for the most powerful job in the world was wanting it. When he was asked early in his campaign why he was qualified to be President, he answered, "I look around me at the others in the race, and I say to myself, 'Well, if they think they can do it, why not me? Why not me?' That's the answer. And I think it's enough." ▪

## ALL IN A DAY'S WORK

**MY FATHER** is a skilled CPA who is not great at self-promotion. So when an advertising salesman offered to put my father's business placard in the shopping carts of a supermarket, my dad jumped at the chance. Fully a year went by before we got a call that could be traced to those placards.

"Richard Larson, CPA?" the caller asked.

"That's right," my father answered. "May I help you?"

"Yes," the voice said. "One of your shopping carts is in my yard, and I want you to come and get it."

-MATTHEW LARSON

**ONE OF MY CO-WORKERS** got a speeding ticket and was attending a defensive-driving course to have points erased from her license. The instructor, a police officer, emphasized that being on time was crucial and that the classroom doors would be locked when each session began.

Just after one class started, someone knocked on the locked door. The officer opened it and asked, "Why are you late?"

The student replied, "I was trying not to get another ticket." The officer let him in.

-PATTY STEFFER

**WHEN I WORKED** for the security department of a large retail store, my duties included responding to fire and burglar alarms. A side door of the building was wired with a security alarm, since it was not supposed to be used by customers. Nevertheless they found the convenience of the exit tempting. Even a sign with large red letters, warning "Alarm will sound if opened," failed to keep people from using it.

One day, after attending to a number of shrieking alarms, I placed a small handmade sign on the door that totally eliminated the problem: "Wet Paint."

-L. J. HINES

**WHEN THE COMPANY** I worked for had an employee-suggestion competition, I told my staff to submit entries that would save money for the firm.

The winner was a man in my department who suggested we post corporate memos on bulletin boards, instead of printing 200 individual copies for distribution. He got a helium balloon with the company logo and one share of stock.

And a memo announcing the prize went out to 200 people.

-KUMIKO YOSHIDA

**I'M A CAPTAIN** with a major airline, and I routinely monitor the flight attendants' announcements while taxiing to the gate. Impatient passengers often stand up and attempt to dash forward before we arrive. Once, instead of the usual terse voice reminding people to remain in their seats, I heard the attendant declare, "In the history of our airline, no passenger has ever beaten the aircraft to the gate. So, ladies and gentlemen, please remain seated."

-JOE CONFORTI

**DURING AN AUTOPSY** I watched when I was a criminal-justice student, the pathologist asked for help from an X-ray technician. A young woman set up the equipment; then we all stepped outside so the picture could be taken. Without thinking, the young woman said to the corpse, "Hold your breath, please." After taking the X-ray, she added, "You can breathe now." There was a pause, and then the pathologist said, "If that guy breathes, I'm out of here."

-RHONDA RIGSBY

# Benny's Heart

## By Lawrence Elliott

When her son's life was torn from her, a mother's grief became unbearable. But a dangerous moment helped her find a reason to live.

Linda Zweigle had two sons and loved both with her whole heart. But Eric was 21 and already his own man, while Benny still came to her beaming a great grin and grabbing her in a big bear hug. The 16-year-old was only an average student at Fresno High in central California,

but to Linda, a single mother who worked at Macy's cosmetics counter, he could do no wrong.

Benny, six-foot-two and still growing, was a standout baseball player who hoped to play pro ball. But lately he'd been caught up in daydreams of having his own car to drive and work on. He loved to tinker with machinery.

Benny's talents were never more apparent than the morning he heard Linda groan, "Oh no!" Their refrigerator had given up the ghost, and a new one was definitely not in the budget. She left for work disconsolate. Benny, pretending he was going to school, doubled back home. It took him all day to take the refrigerator apart, piece by piece, doctor the malfunction and then put it back together. But by the time Linda came home, it was purring.

"You fixed it," she gasped. Benny smiled shyly. Then she understood. "You cut school." He nodded.

"Are you mad at me?" he asked. This time it was Linda who grabbed him in a bear hug. Her Benny had golden hands and a good heart. In time he would find himself and settle down.

**It was not to be. On Friday, September 17, 1993,** Benny left after dark to meet his friends at the neighborhood hangout, the brightly lit lot across from the Zweigles' house.

At a little before 9:30 p.m. a Cadillac rolled by the lot and taunts were exchanged. Twenty minutes later the Cadillac returned, this time with the front-seat passenger leveling a gun and firing four shots from the open window. Benny was hit behind the right ear and fell like a stone, facedown.

His brother, Eric, ran into the street at the sound of the shots. He saw boys scattering. Someone shouted, "They shot Benny!"

Eric fell to his knees by the crumpled body, saw the gathering pool of blood by his brother's head, heard his brother's insubstantial breathing.

"Somebody call 911!" he begged as he ran to get his mother and then raced back to take Benny's hand. "You're gonna be okay, bro," he said over and over. But Linda took one look and knew otherwise.

When she next saw her boy, he was in an intensive care unit, attached to a welter of tubes and monitors. He seemed to be asleep. But a doctor showed Linda the brain scan and explained that the bullet had spun around inside Benny's head; his brain looked like shattered glass. It was dead, the doctor said, and without artificial support, his heart and lungs would fail, too. What did she want to do? Nothing, she said. She wanted her son back.

Hours passed. Night turned into gray dawn as Linda tried to come to terms with her loss. Her Benny would never become a man, would never realize the potential of his God-given gifts. She had never felt such an agonizing hurt of body and soul. She thought, *How can a mother recover from such a loss?*

Someone asked her to meet with counselors from the California Transplant Donor Network. They tried to console her, explaining that through her, Benny could give life and sight to others by donating his healthy organs. Scarcely understanding, she turned away, wondering what good cutting into her Benny would do.

Yet, unaccountably, she said yes. Was it to keep Benny's spirit alive? Or to give a young boy like Benny the chance to realize his potential? She didn't know, but gave permission for Benny's corneas, pancreas, liver, kidneys, lungs, bone marrow and heart to be removed, recognizing that they would go to people she was never to know.

At 4:45 p.m. the coroner pronounced Benjamin Anthony Zweigle dead. Linda went home thinking that a heart must somehow be connected to the soul. In the long nights to come, she often wondered who had gotten her Benny's soul.

**The following morning, near the town of Modesto** 90 miles away, 60-year-old Lyle Baade woke thankful for one more day on earth. He'd suffered three major heart attacks and had twice had open-heart surgery. He lived with almost constant chest pain and could no longer help out on the family walnut farm.

He went on the list for a compatible heart at Stanford University Medical Center. Some on the list were lucky, but Lyle came to know others who had died waiting. He himself had been called twice, only to be bitterly disappointed.

One time, already prepped for surgery, he was told that the donor heart was bruised and unusable. Then, just a week ago, when he and his wife, Beverly, had taken a drive to the ocean, the pager linking him to Stanford, which he wore even to bed, had somehow failed to beep. By the time he heard the urgent messages on his telephone answering machine—"We have a heart for you! Please get back to us!"—it was too late.

But that Sunday, September 19, as he and Beverly left for church, the pager beeped with word that there was a heart for him. At the hospital, there was barely time for Beverly's hurried kiss before Lyle was whisked away to surgery, where his enlarged, overworked heart was removed and the healthy, fist-size donor heart was sutured to his aorta and pulmonary artery. It needed no jump-start; it began beating at once.

As soon as Lyle was fully awake, he realized he was a different man. He asked for a stethoscope and listened to the firm thump-thump-thump of the new heart, so unlike the faltering, squishy sound his poor sick one had made. Once home he walked so briskly that Beverly had to run to keep up. He raked leaves. He went back to his hobbies of camping and building furniture.

Lyle knew almost from the start whose heart had saved his life. Given his medical file to take to his doctor in Modesto, he saw that the donor was a 16-year-old from Fresno who had died of a gunshot wound. A check of the newspapers, which turned up Benny Zweigle's obituary, told the rest of the story.

Because donor information is supposed to be kept confidential, Lyle did not contact Linda Zweigle directly. But he

did send her an unsigned message through the donor network expressing his everlasting gratitude.

**There was little for Linda Zweigle to be thankful for** after Benny's murder. She did everything she had to do—she went to work, cleaned house, prepared meals—but it was as though she were someone else. The real Linda Zweigle was constantly waiting to hear the door bang open and the sound of her Benny shouting, "Hey, Mom, I'm home!"

Then came the anonymous letter. It was from the man who had gotten Benny's heart; he wanted to thank her. Linda was shaken by the news. A 60-year-old man. Why had they given Benny's heart to someone whose life was nearly over? Her hope that the heart had gone to a boy or girl with a whole life to live—the life that had been stolen from Benny—was shattered.

Even the arrest and conviction of the teenage boys responsible for Benny's death brought little peace to her. Tried as juveniles, they would be freed to start new lives when they turned 25, while Benny slept on in his grave.

**Meanwhile, Lyle and Beverly Baade** had moved to the retirement community of Ventana Lakes near Phoenix, where they were leading happy, active lives. On the afternoon of April 19, 2000, they were in a meeting of the residents that kept droning on. Lyle had to get to a 2:45 appointment for his annual check-up, so he and Beverly quietly rose from their seats.

But as they walked to the exit, a huge bearded man stopped them. It was Richard Glassel, a local crank who'd had run-ins with his neighbors. "Go back and sit down," he growled, shoving Lyle hard.

Stunned, Lyle looked down to see that the man was holding a pistol. He drew Beverly behind him and watched as Glassel moved away from them.

"He's got a gun!" Lyle yelled.

"I'm going to kill you all!" Glassel called out as he began firing.

Lyle pulled Beverly behind a partition as he saw friends topple from their chairs and heard the cries of the wounded. People dropped to the floor, desperately scrabbling for shelter.

Suddenly the gunfire stopped. Glassel laid down the pistol and raised an assault rifle. *He really is going to kill us all,* Lyle thought. Then it was as though he were hearing a voice from outside himself, and it was saying, *You can take this guy. You can get there before he turns that rifle on you. Do it!*

Lyle came flying out of a crouch as if he were still the teenage linebacker of his high school football team and launched into a flying tackle that brought the 300-pound Glassel down in a heap. But the gunman fought back in a rage, clawing at Lyle with one hand and scrambling for the rifle with the other.

Glassel got his finger on the rifle trigger and pulled. In the echo of its roar, a victim cried out. But then Lyle slammed the rifle to the floor and pinned it. The burly gunman writhed and heaved, but Lyle managed to hold Glassel to the ground until others wrestled the rifle away, pinned down his wrists and tied his ankles.

When the police arrived, they found that Glassel had enough ammunition to kill everyone in the community center three times over. As it was, two residents were dead and three wounded. Those who survived were saved only because of Lyle. His hand had been clawed bloody by the frenzied gunman, but Benny's heart beat steadily.

> # Linda Zweigle was constantly waiting to hear the door bang open and the sound of Benny shouting, "Hey, Mom, I'm home."

Lyle's daughter, Tammi Bowman, moved by the outpouring of gratitude from people he had saved or their loved ones, decided it was time Benny Zweigle's mother knew who had gotten her son's heart. She leaked the story to Kimi Yoshino, a Fresno *Bee* reporter.

At first Linda didn't want to hear it. "Anything you tell me is just going to make me cry," she told Yoshino. But then it sank in: The old grandfather who was walking around with her Benny's heart had saved 41 people from violent death.

For Linda, that changed everything. It was as though she had been freed of a great weight. She read the newspaper story again and again, always with tears in her eyes. But now they were tears of pride and joy. Benny's organs had saved many lives. But it was his heart that had rescued even more and spared their families the grief she'd borne these seven years.

And at that moment, Benny's death, which haunted her as senseless and useless, seemed to have meaning. She would never stop missing him, but her loss became somehow bearable. She believes it was Benny's voice Lyle heard that day, and in her heart, she knows what happened to Benny's soul. ∎

# *Unforgettable*

By Billy Martin
with
Mark Kram
~

The most colorful manager in baseball history won seven World Series with the Yankees. Then, at 72, he took charge of the Mets, proclaiming, "Most people my age are dead. And you could look it up."

# Casey Stengel

Seldom has there been a more implausible figure. For nearly 60 years, Charles Dillon Stengel, better known as Casey, duck-walked through baseball, ruffling the preen of some players, salving the hurt of hundreds of others and all the while thoroughly abusing the native tongue. His favorite phrase was, "You could look it up!", his favorite description, "Fairly amazin'!" His favorite place was in a dugout, and come to think of it he always looked funny out of a baseball uniform. Little wonder. Casey Stengel was a baseball man. For more than half a century, he ate, slept and drank the game of baseball.

The first time I ever saw Casey was in the winter of 1945, when he was managing the minor-league Oakland Acorns and overseeing team tryouts. I was a skinny 17-year-old, with a big nose, a ragged

uniform and a desperate desire to play baseball. Casey was 55, his face weathered to a craggy profile like the side of a mountain. His wizened body seemed the work of a crazed sculptor. I remember being in awe of him—perhaps because it was he who would say whether or not I had a future in baseball.

That first day, Casey ignored me. But the next morning, he began hitting ground balls to me, over and over again until there were blisters on his hands. "This kid won't quit," he said. "He's gonna be a player." We developed a spontaneous bond that day—one that would last the remaining years of his life.

And what fairly amazin' years they were! For here was a man who, in his first 25 years as a minor- and major-league manager, had not notably distinguished himself, finishing no higher than fifth in an eight-team league during one ten-year stretch. Yet, at 59, this consistent also-ran was named manager of the New York Yankees. And in the 12 seasons that followed, he ran up a stunning record of ten pennants and seven World Series championships. The gnarled old clown, baseball's gadfly, the game's freest spirit, had become an irrevocable success. And there was more: At 72, he became manager of the infant and mad-comic New York Mets and threw up the first beams for the team that would become one of the zaniest success stories in baseball history. "Most people my age," he said, taking the job, "are dead. And you could look it up."

If any manager can ever be called a genius, Casey Stengel is that man. Unless it was convenient, his memory was faultless—as clear and specific as the ring of a bell on a still day. It was the gift, the switch that he pulled to maneuver his players on and off the field, and it made him a master in the subtle game of using a certain batter against a certain pitcher, of putting a strong arm in the right position. This is called "platooning," and the old man was the father of it; baseball would never be the same again.

Casey Stengel was born in Kansas City, Mo., in 1890. From the day his father signed his consent for the boy to play professional ball, young Stengel would be known as the man from K.C., hence the name "Casey." At 19, he was playing for Maysville, Ky., where he used to practice slides in the outfield between innings.

"Keep tryin', son," said one of the veterans of the club, "and you'll soon be up *there*." "In the majors, you mean?" asked Stengel. "No, up there!" said the veteran pointing to a mental hospital beyond centerfield.

Though Casey had wanted to be a dentist (he spent three years at Western Dental College in Kansas City), in the summer of 1912, while he was playing for the Montgomery team in the Southern Association, his head turned completely toward the big leagues. It all happened one day when major-league shortstop Kid Elberfeld stopped by to watch Casey play.

The Kid's eyes pinned on Casey's valise. "That's a thousand-miler if the weather stays good," said the Kid. "But if it rains, you'll find yourself holding nothing but the handles. Buy yourself a good one. You'll need it if you're going to be a

big-leaguer. And don't worry, you will be. You can forget about pulling teeth; you're made for this game."

That fall, new bag and all, Casey was called up to the Brooklyn Trolley Dodgers. He would remember Kid Elberfeld's encouragement and help him later, for he was never to forget a friend. He used to send money quietly to old players, down on their luck. "Is it true," I once asked him, "that you just sent $1,000 to some old ballplayer in Tacoma?"

"Mind your own business, Martin!" he shot back with a faint smile on his face. "You might be sittin' in a rockin' chair someday on the porch of some nursing home. Come to think of it, you belong in one now."

For 14 years, Casey played for five National League teams. Though only a fair player, he took more than his share of the fickle limelight. After hitting his second game-winning home run against the Yanks in the 1923 Giants-Yankees World Series, for example, he thumbed his nose at pitcher Sam Jones, then at the entire Yankee bench.

"I am horrified!" roared Yankee owner Col. Jacob Ruppert, who was disturbed that his spanking-new stadium had been desecrated by such a vulgar act. He requested that baseball commissioner Kenesaw Mountain Landis take disciplinary action. Judge Landis refused. "Stengel," the commissioner explained to Ruppert, "is Stengel."

I often recall that retort. Stengel was Stengel, but what was he really? No one will ever agree to the answer. To me, growing up in a tough section of Oakland, a lost and lonesome kid from the streets who never had a real father, Casey *was* a father. To some players, especially those who did not like being platooned, he was an upstaging meddler. To his Yankee general manager George Weiss, Casey was a man who gave 24 hours a day to his job. To Branch Rickey, famous manager and executive in both major leagues, he was "the perfect link between the team and the public."

No team ever needed that link more than the Yankees when Casey became their manager in 1949. The fans admired us (I joined the team a year later as a second baseman), but they had also lost interest in us.

Now here came Casey Stengel, regarded as baseball's funniest manager. It was first thought that he was hired to humor the public, but Stengel, with his special touch, made 1949 a memorable year. The fifteenth manager in the Yanks' 46-year history did the greatest glue-and-tape job ever seen; he also made the Yankees human.

"We had 72 injuries during Casey's first season," trainer Gus Mauch likes to recall. "Even Joe DiMaggio missed half of our games. But Casey juggled the lineups, and before we knew it we had defeated the Boston Red Sox for the pennant and taken the World Series from the Dodgers. Casey did it with mirrors."

Throughout that season and for the next 11, the public would see a legend grow, and the Yankees themselves would see a manager evolve who was more than a match for their image. Unmatched, too, was Casey's language. It was almost impossible for anyone to unwind the tangle of clauses and tenses that issued from him with machine-gun rapidity.

Yet the elongated narratives without proper names—Stengelese it was called—held audiences spellbound in hotel lobbies and dugouts across the country. Once, grappling with the problem of one young player, he suddenly rose up in the dugout and began waving his arms: "That feller runs splendid, but he needs help at the plate, which coming from the country chasing rabbits all winter give him strong legs, although he broke one falling out of a tree, which shows you can't tell, and when a curve ball comes he waves at it, and if the pitchers don't throw curves you have no pitching staff, so how is a manager going to know whether to tell boys to fall out of trees and break legs so he can run fast even if he can't hit a curve ball."

Most wives might flinch at such baffling monologues or be embarrassed by a husband like Casey. But not Edna, whom he married in 1924. To her credit, she never tried to remake him. Visually, they were a curious couple. Tall, handsome and striking, Edna always seemed to belong to someone else rather than this crusty, tobacco-stained character whose curled-over shuffle made him look like a man whose vest was buttoned to his pants.

As manager of the Yanks, Casey whipped, pacified and conned toward excellence some of the most luminous stars ever seen in baseball. Some say he was a master psychologist, but I believe that he simply really *knew* men, knew what was in their hearts and their minds, their fears, their peccadilloes. As shortstop Phil Rizzuto used to say, "He could look into your eyes and tell if you were going to get a base hit."

Casey liked to say that he was a mother hen and that we were his chicks. But he always made sure the credit for his success went to the players, and I never heard him blow his own horn. When reporters would ask the secret of his success, Casey would reply with a question: "I couldn't have done it with football players, could I?"

Eventually, however, Casey's dominance over the Yankees began to weaken. The front office—torn by politics and no longer under the hard hand of George Weiss—interfered with his decisions. The other clubs in the league, so long the victims, started to improve. Looking for an excuse, the Yankee owners began saying that Casey was too old.

When the Yanks lost the 1960 Series to the Pirates, Casey's fate was sealed. The game's unlikely blend of Donald Duck and Charles de Gaulle was fired—at 70. No more would we have to contend with his crazed syntax; no more would we see that waddle to the mound that became his trademark.

Then, almost as suddenly as he was fired, the Old Perfesser, as he had become known to many, was hired as the manager of the New York Mets, an expansion team that was so bad that one day Casey would throw up his arms, look into the sky and plead, "Can't anybody here play this game?" But Casey made an abject loser endearing, and it became an "in" thing to be a Met fan.

He managed the club for three years, retiring at 75. The following year, he was elected to baseball's Hall of Fame.

The next years of his life were spent quietly at his home in Glendale, Calif. He followed the box scores each day and now and then would journey to an oldtimers' game. We kept in touch by phone, and other friends would call occasionally.

Still, for all the calls, Casey was lonely. Edna was in a nursing home, living in a world where Casey did not exist. During these days, Casey was taken care of by a tenaciously loyal housekeeper. Often, he would spend time with her 9-year-old grandson, talking of Mantle, Maris and Berra, all of the

> Casey liked to say he was a mother hen. He always made sure the credit for his success went to his players.

stars, all the days that had drifted far into shadows. Sometimes, waving his arms weakly, he would teach the neighborhood youngsters how to slide and play with them on the lawn.

One of the last times I saw him was in 1974 at an oldtimers' game in Texas, and I could see the excitement in his eyes. As he went onto the field to a standing ovation, he did a little jig that brought the house down. On September 29, 1975, Casey died of cancer at the age of 85.

His funeral was the saddest moment of my life. After the service, I walked through his house, past all the mementos of the old man's life. There were pictures of Casey with emperors and kings—all remnants of a career that began in the horse-and-buggy era and ended with him shepherding his players across the country in Boeing 727 jetliners.

As I walked out of the house, I thought of the awful rent that would be left in the fabric of baseball by Casey's passing. I remember what New York's Gov. Hugh Carey had said the day after his death: "Casey Stengel had the baseball mind of a genius, the heart of Santa Claus and St. Francis and the face of a clown. Something very good has gone from our lives." So it has. ∎

# Going the Distance:

## Face to Face *with* CHRISTOPHER REEVE

He remained optimistic when he took part in this interview just months before his death. And he had high hopes that the work he had done to help support research and rehabilitation centers would pay off, not only for him but for everyone trying to live with paralysis.

*By Alanna Nash*

I
t doesn't feel like a hospital here, does it?" says Christopher Reeve, his eyes sweeping the office in the quietly elegant home that he shares with his wife, Dana, and their 12-year-old son, Will. "That's because Dana, from the very beginning, wanted our family to live as normal a life as possible."

The "beginning" was May 27, 1995, the day the athletic actor, an accomplished rider, approached a routine three-foot jump in a Virginia horse show. His chestnut Thoroughbred balked and stopped short, and Reeve, his hands tangled in the bridle, catapulted headfirst onto the ground.

The injury rendered Reeve, now 52, a quadriplegic, confined to a ventilator and a wheelchair—and initially contemplating suicide.

But he titled his second memoir *Nothing Is Impossible* and has spent the years since proving that point. Reeve works fiercely on his rehabilitation and has regained sensation over 70 percent of his body. He can go for long periods without his ventilator (he had electrodes implanted in his abdomen to help him breathe on his own). And he has stunned doctors by willing himself to move one of his fingers and, in water, his legs and arms.

Reeve has labored tirelessly on legislation for spinal cord injury patients: His Christopher Reeve Paralysis Act goes before Congress this fall. And he hasn't put his creative life aside either. A&E will soon air his second directorial project, "The Brooke Ellison Story," the real-life saga of an 11-year-old girl paralyzed from the neck down as the result of an auto accident.

Dressed in a striped polo shirt, white duck pants and running shoes, Reeve spoke with *Reader's Digest* about the film, his advocacy and his remarkable journey. On the rebound from a recent hospital stay, he displayed his usual tenacity, saying, "Your body is not who you are. The mind and spirit transcend the body."

**RD: It's been more than nine years since the accident. How has it changed your perspective on life?**
**Reeve:** I have more awareness of other people and, I hope, more sensitivity to their needs. I also find that I'm more direct and outspoken. It's important to me to say what I really mean.

**RD: In your second book, you wrote about feeling angry after the accident. Have you accepted things now?**
**Reeve:** I don't get angry, because it wouldn't do any good. I experience frustration sometimes, such as when I have a crisis, like I just did.

**RD: What happened?**
**Reeve:** I've had three bad life-threatening infections this year. This most recent was a blood infection caused by an abrasion on my left hip that I probably picked up one day when I was on the exercise bike. It seemed benign but developed into strep. Then a lot of major organs shut down. We're trying to figure out what's going on.

Before that one, I got a severe infection in New Orleans just a few days before shooting the movie. I was frustrated: "This is not fair; come on. Let's not fall apart. I've come too far." So sometimes I get jealous of people who take their ability to move for granted.

**RD: Do you get scared?**
**Reeve:** No, I don't

**RD: How could you not?**
**Reeve:** It's a proven fact that you can control panic by applying rational processes. In all my days of flying and sailing and riding, every now and again I got myself into a jam.

On Christmas Day in 1985 I was flying over the Green Mountains in Vermont. Thick clouds, snowing. And the

"Sometimes I get jealous of people who take their ability to move for granted," said Reeve, shown here with his son Will and wife Dana.

warning light went on. I looked out and saw oil all over the wing. I knew I had to shut down that engine and fly to Boston on the other.

You're hoping it doesn't develop a problem, too. But the chance of a multi-engine failure is very, very remote. Literally, you use your brain to stop panic. I've had a lot of training in that area from my life before the injury.

**RD: It's almost as if everything in your life up to the accident was preparation for this phase.**
**Reeve:** That's probably true. I'm glad I didn't know it at the time.

**RD: So what's the latest product of your determination, in terms of regaining movement and sensation?**

**Reeve:** There hasn't been any new recovery since what was published in 2002. But I've been able to maintain most of what I achieved.

**RD: Are you still optimistic you will walk again?**
**Reeve:** I am optimistic. But I also know that, with time, I'm beginning to fight issues of aging as well as long-term paralysis. So it seems more difficult to project than it was five years ago. But I haven't given up.

**RD: Has there been a change in your optimism?**
**Reeve:** Hope, to me, must be based—now knowing as much as I do—on a projection derived from solid data. But, yes, there's been a change in my state of mind, because in May of next year it will be ten years [since the accident], and I doubt if by that time there's going

to be a procedure suitable for me. At 52, knowing that a safe trial for me may still be years away has changed my perspective. I didn't think it would take this long.

**RD: What's been the hardest part?**
**Reeve:** Watching the slow progress of research in this country. I don't know if it would have made me walk sooner, but I would have had the satisfaction of knowing we're all on the same page. Groups of people who have differences about all kinds of issues are united to fight against AIDS. Wouldn't it be great if we were as united about biomedical research for diseases that affect 128 million Americans?

**RD: Tell me about the Christopher Reeve Paralysis Act.**
**Reeve:** It's broken into three parts. One is for biomedical research. The other is rehabilitation research. The third is for quality-of-life programs. It would create five centers across the country, to make sure that there is support for people living with paralysis. Patients do better the sooner you get them up and moving. Put them in pools, on treadmills, on exercise bikes—anything to keep the systems of the body from breaking down. No magic pill will cure spinal cord injury. It'll be a combination of drug therapy, or procedure, plus rehabilitation.

**RD: Does the Act have broad support?**
**Reeve:** I'm quite optimistic that it will pass, because there's nothing controversial about it. It doesn't even mention embryonic stem cells.

**RD: What's your position on embryonic stem cell research?**
**Reeve:** I advocate it because I think scientists should be free to pursue every possible avenue. It appears, though, at the moment, that embryonic stem cells are effective in treating acute injuries and are not able to do much about chronic injuries.

**RD: How have political decisions slowed stem cell research?**
**Reeve:** The religious right has had quite an influence on the debate. I don't think that's appropriate. When we're setting public policy, no one segment of society deserves the only seat at the table. That's the way it's set in the Constitution. So debate all we want, hear from everybody. And then allow our representatives to weigh the factors and make laws that are going to be ethically

sound, moral, responsible, but not the result of undue pressure from any particular entity.

**RD: Is it hard to be patient?**
**Reeve:** I've lasted more than nine years, so I can wait a little longer. I also realize that a lot of people are watching me, to see what I'm going to do. I want to make sure I'm making a smart choice. I'm not at a point of desperation where I'd say, "Just somebody fix me, anywhere."

**RD: Did you ever feel that way?**
**Reeve:** I was much more impatient five years ago. I started out saying, "What do you mean you can't fix the

> "I think we all have a little voice inside us that will guide us. It will tell us the right thing to do. It may be God, I don't know."

spinal cord?" I remember telling a neurosurgeon, "Don't give me too much information, because at the moment my ignorance is my best asset." Then, over time, as you learn more about the complexities of the central nervous system, and you learn to balance your life—even to get a life back—your perspective changes.

**RD: You've talked people out of suicide who've just suffered the kind of injury you had. How do you do it?**
**Reeve:** I tell them about a lot of things that are available, what's happening with research, particularly for the acute phase of injury, and what opportunities there are for rehabilitation. And I tell them that even though you can't imagine building a new life now, you need to wait until everything stops spinning and you can look at it more clearly. In the meantime, don't do anything rash.

I haven't lost anybody yet. And it probably happens, gosh, sometimes as much as once a week.

**RD: You went nearly 50 years without religion in your life. What made you recently join the Unitarian Church?**
**Reeve:** It gives me a moral compass. I often refer to Abe Lincoln, who said, "When I do good, I feel good. When I do bad, I feel bad. And that is my religion." I think we all have a little voice inside us that will guide us. It may be God, I don't know. But I think that if we shut out all the noise and clutter from our lives and listen to that voice, it will tell us the right thing to do. The Unitarian believes that God is good and believes that God believes that man is good. Inherently. The Unitarian God is not a God of vengeance. And that is something I can appreciate.

**RD: What kinds of exercises are you doing now to regain movement?**
**Reeve:** I haven't been able to do as much as I did before. Normally I would spend three to four hours in the morning and maybe two hours at night exercising. The program is centered around the bike. Electrodes are attached to my leg muscles, and as they fire, they innervate the muscles to spin the wheel. Then I do something called E-Stim. Electrodes are placed on the major muscle groups, and as they fire, they work the muscles. That's how I've been able to keep up my strength.

**RD: What really keeps you going?**
**Reeve:** The love and support of my family, and the fact that I'm needed. I'm working. I focus on the opportunities that come my way rather than on the things that haven't arrived yet.

**RD: Tell us about "The Brooke Ellison Story."**
**Reeve:** It is a remarkable story of somebody with a severe disability who's determined not to be left back. I felt that if I could find one compelling story about a family coping with spinal cord injury and creating a new life in spite of it, I wanted to do that one film—and then go off and make a comedy and not feel guilty! I hope it will do more than all the speeches I've given to raise awareness about spinal cord injury and disability in general.

**RD: What has been the biggest loss as a result of your condition?**
**Reeve:** The loss of freedom as I used to understand it. I still have creative freedom, and I have basic freedom, but not the way it used to be.

**RD: And what's the biggest gift?**
**Reeve:** The growth of our family, the support we give each other—my two oldest kids, and Will, and of course Dana, who is by my side no matter what. And that's really extraordinary.

**RD: How has this changed your relationship with your wife?**
**Reeve:** I think it drew us even closer.

**RD: What's the first thing you would do if you regained movement tomorrow?**
**Reeve:** Complete movement? Restored to normal? Mmmmm ... Take full advantage of having complete freedom back again. And you can read between the lines! ■

# LIFE'S LIKE THAT

**LOW ON GAS** while on a vacation trip to Las Vegas, I pulled my van into a service station. As I was turning in, I spied lying on the ground a gas cap that looked like it might replace my missing one.

I hurriedly parked by the pump, jumped out of the van, ran over and picked up the cap. I was pleasantly surprised to find that it screwed easily onto my tank. A perfect fit, I thought.

And then I noticed the keyhole in the top of the cap.

-BOB SJOSTRAND, PORTERVILLE, CALIF.

**WHILE WAITING** for a friend, I saw a meter maid ticketing cars. I glanced over at the car next to me and noticed the time had elapsed in its meter. I put in a quarter.

I was smugly thinking, That's one driver who won't be getting a ticket, when the meter maid got in the car and drove off.

-DOROTHY COYNER, ALBUQUERQUE, N.M.

**MY FRIEND** is notorious for waiting until the needle is on empty before filling his gas tank. Finally his car died on him, and we had to push it to the nearest filling station. After my friend finished pumping gas, the attendant asked if he had learned anything.

"Yeah," my friend muttered, "I learned I have a 15-gallon tank."

-EDWARD HYATT, IRVINE, CALIF.

*By James Michener*

# You Never STOP Learning

His experiences in the war confirmed what he had always believed: Education provides "the self-discipline that keeps man driving toward hard and distant goals."

ILLUSTRATION BY TIM BOWER

The war had passed us by on Guadalcanal in 1945, and we could see certain victory ahead. Relieved of pressure, our top officers in the South Pacific Force could have been excused if they loafed, but the ones I knew well did not. One carrier admiral used his free time to study everything he could get on tank warfare. The head of our outfit, Vice Adm. William Lowndes Calhoun, spent six hours a day learning French.

I asked him, "Admiral, what's the big deal with French?"

"How do I know where I'll be sent when the war's over?" he replied.

A few nights later someone asked, "By the way, Michener, what are you studying?" The question, though probably an idle one, stunned me, and the challenge touched off a profound response. That very night I started work on an idea that I had been toying with for months. In a lantern-lit, mosquito-filled tin shack, I began writing *Tales of the South Pacific*.

The good work of the world is accomplished principally by people who dedicate themselves unstintingly to the big, distant goal. Weeks, months, years pass, but the good workman knows he is gambling on an ultimate achievement, one that cannot be measured by time spent. Responsible men and women leap to the challenge of these jobs that require years to fulfill and are happiest when so involved. But this means that if they hope to make a real contribution, they must re-educate themselves periodically. Otherwise they are doomed to mediocrity.

In the United States the average man (leave out doctors and specialized scientists) can expect to work in three radically different fields before he retires. The lawyer is dragged into business reorganization and winds up a college president. The engineer uses his slide rule for a while, then finds himself a sales expert and ends up in labor relations. The schoolteacher becomes a principal; later on he heads an automobile agency.

I have been typical in that I have had widely scattered jobs: teacher, businessman, soldier, traveler, writer. No college education could give me specific preparation for any of these jobs. But by fantastic luck, I got to Swarthmore College just as it was launching an experiment. At the end of my sophomore year, the faculty told a group of us, "Life does not consist of taking courses in small segments. We are going to turn you loose on some huge tasks. Let's see what you can do with them."

We were excused from all class attendance and were told, "Pick out three fields that interest you." I chose logic, English history and the novel. "Go to the library and learn what you can. At the end of two years, we'll bring in some experts from Harvard and Yale, and they will determine whether you have educated yourself."

What followed was an experience in intellectual grandeur. The Swarthmore professors, realizing that my testing would be a test of them, too, helped me gain as thorough a knowledge of those three fields as a young man could absorb. When the two years ended, the visiting experts for a week queried, probed and heckled. At the end, one of the examiners said to me simply, "You have the beginnings of a real education."

He was right: It was only the beginnings. Nothing I studied in college has been of direct use to me in my various occupations. But what I did learn was how to learn, how to organize, how to educate myself. And since then, experience and observation have taught me that it is not so much the original education that counts: it's the re-education—the self-discipline that keeps man driving toward hard and distant goals, the human values he believes in.

I remember four of us would-be officers shivering in our shorts in the room. A grim-faced selection committee asked, "What can you do?"

Specialization is not enough. For the big jobs—historically, culturally, morally—what the world needs is well-rounded human beings.

I remember a day in 1942 when the U.S. Navy was hungry for talent. Four of us would-be officers were shivering in our shorts in a small room. A grim-faced selection committee asked, "What can you do?" and the first man replied, "I'm a buyer for Macy's, and I've trained myself to judge very quickly between markets and prices and trends." The board replied, "Can't you do anything practical?" And they shunted him off to one side.

The next man was a lawyer. He had to confess, "I can weigh evidence and organize information." He was rejected.

I was the third, and when I answered, "I know language and a good deal of history," the board groaned, and I went shivering away.

Then the fourth man said boldly, "I'm a college-trained engineer, and I can overhaul diesel engines."

The committee practically embraced him and made him an officer on the spot.

But this is not the end of the story. When the war was over, the Macy's buyer was assistant to the Secretary of the Navy, in charge of many complex responsibilities requiring instant good judgment. He had given himself courses in Naval management and government procedures and had become a top expert. The lawyer wound up as assistant to Admiral Halsey and, in a crucial battle, deduced logically from intelligence reports just where the Japanese fleet had to be. He came out covered with medals.

I got the job of Naval secretary to several Congressional committees who were determining the future of America in the South Pacific.

What was the engineer doing at the end of the war? He was still overhauling diesel engines. ■

# ALL IN A DAY'S WORK

**ON HIS FIRST MORNING** delivering newspapers, my son was riding with his supervisor, who was showing him some tricks of the trade. He proceeded to demonstrate how to throw a newspaper accurately.

"Now remember," he warned, "it's 5:30 in the morning, so you don't want to make a big ruckus. This customer likes his paper right on his front porch."

The supervisor then hurled the paper toward the house. It landed on the customer's car and set off the alarm.

-NYLA LOLOTAI

**WHEN I WORKED** in airline reservations, we had an executive desk, which did bookings for corporate clients during the day. One evening the phone rang and rang. Finally our supervisor picked it up and said in a monotone, "We are open from 8 a.m. to 5 p.m. Please call back then."

A voice on the other end asked, "Is this a recording?"

Without thinking, my boss replied, "Yes, it is."

-ANNETTE MURRAY

**MY PROBLEM** is getting to work on time. One morning while driving to the office I came across a turtle in the middle of the road. I just had to rescue the creature. It took a few minutes for me to stop the car, grab the turtle and move it off to the side. Then I rushed on to work.

When I saw my boss at the door, I said quickly, "It's not my fault, Rich. There was a turtle in the road."

Before I could go any further, he bellowed, "So what—you drove behind it?"

-CHRISTY STEINBRUNNER

**WALKING THROUGH** the hallways at the middle school where I work, I saw a new substitute teacher standing outside his classroom with his forehead against a locker. I heard him mutter, "How did you get yourself into this?"

Knowing he was assigned to a difficult class, I tried to offer moral support. "Are you okay?" I asked. "Can I help?"

He lifted his head and replied, "I'll be fine as soon as I get this kid out of his locker."

-HELEN BUTTON

**AS AN INNKEEPER** in Vermont, I meet a lot of different people. One morning at breakfast, I had a nice talk with one of my guests, an Englishman. I mentioned some British phrases that I thought were strange: "I'll do it straightaway," "He's backward about coming forward," and "Don't get your knickers in a twist."

My English guest stared at me for a moment, then responded, "I don't care how many cowboys you have in America, I still don't see how you can shoot the breeze."

-KRISHNA K. DASARAKOTHAPALLI

# Triplets ...And They Didn't Know It!

ILLUSTRATION BY SARAH WILKINS

Bobby, David and Eddy had lived their young lives thinking that something was missing. They were very smart, but all of them had trouble at school. Bobby kept dreaming about "a kid who looked like me."

By
*Phyllis
Battelle*
~

**A**ll his life, 19-year-old Robert Shafran sensed he was special. He had no idea why he felt this way, although he knew he had a near-genius I.Q. of 148 and recognized that he was an irrepressible extrovert. Adults sometimes sighed, "Bobby, when they made you, they broke the mold." Bobby rather liked that; it appealed to his quirky sense of humor and strong sense of individuality. Yet he had a recurring dream "about a kid who looked like me, talked like me and acted like me." When he woke from it, his feelings of being special were strongly reinforced.

As a teenager, Bobby saw psychiatrists in an attempt to discover why his school performance was falling short of his obvious potential. Their conclusion: It had something to do with his having been adopted as an infant. He dismissed that theory, knowing that his adoptive parents, a Scarsdale, N.Y., physician and his attorney wife, "gave me all the love and support I could ever want." And indeed they did.

"Bobby didn't say a word until he was four," says Elsa Shafran, now retired. "But when he began to speak, it was in long and articulate sentences." Dr. Morton Shafran adds fondly, "He was always precocious but also restless and hyperkinetic." These qualities set him somewhat apart from the world, as though something was missing inside him. Last autumn, Bobby discovered what it was.

On September 3, Bobby enrolled as a freshman at Sullivan County Community College in upstate New York. After he had checked into his dormitory, he began circulating on campus. "I'm gregarious," he explains, "and I was saying, 'Hello, how are you?' to everyone in sight."

Suddenly some students were slapping his back: "Hey, Eddy, how you doin'?"

Bobby grinned. "Fine, guys. But I'm not Eddy."

"Sure you're not—you joker."

Next day the phenomenon continued. "It got increasingly fascinating. Girls were hugging me and calling me Eddy," he recalls. He showed them his driver's license, proving he was Robert Shafran, but that left them unconvinced. One even told him where a birthmark was located on his body—an intimate spot. He was stunned.

**The second night, a student named Michael Domnitz** walked into his room, asking, "Is this 11-C?"

"Yeah."

"Are you"—and at that point Bobby turned around and saw his visitor's face go totally white. "He just stared at me, freaked out. Then he asked, 'Were you adopted?' When I nodded, he asked when I was born, and I told him July 12, 1961. 'Where?' Long Island Jewish-Hillside Medical Center. He grabbed my arm and said, 'Come with me. I've got to show you some pictures!'"

They rushed to another dorm where Domnitz pulled out a snapshot of his best friend, Eddy Galland, who had attended the school the year before, then transferred to another community college near his home in New Hyde Park, N.Y., on Long Island. Now it was Bobby's turn to freak out. "What I saw was a photograph of myself," he says in a hushed voice. "It was like looking in a mirror. It was unmistakably me. I didn't know what to say or do."

Domnitz picked up the phone and began dialing.

Eddy Galland remembers wondering, when the phone rang at 9 p.m., whether it was another weird call from acquaintances upstate "who had been spending their allowances all day to tell me, 'Hey, there's somebody here who looks exactly like you.' Then Mike put Bobby on the phone. Bobby said, 'Eddy, I think you're my twin brother.' I said very calmly, 'Yeah?' Then he said, 'Listen, I've got the same eyes, same nose, same hair, and we were born at the same hospital the same day.'"

The two made arrangements to meet that weekend. But then Bobby decided he couldn't wait. "I told Mike, 'I've got to see Eddy tonight!' And we both got in my car and drove three hours to the Galland home."

At 2 a.m. they knocked on Eddy's door. "It seemed forever," Bobby recalls, "before the door opened. After that, I said, 'Oh, my God'—and simultaneously *saw* myself saying, 'Oh, my God.' I scratched my head—and saw myself scratching my head. I turned away and saw myself turning away. Everything in unison, as though professional mimes were doing this. We started shaking hands and wound up hugging."

In the words of both young men, there was "an instantaneous feeling of love."

That early morning, in the Galland living room, the two brothers quickly noticed other similarities. Both smoked the same brand of cigarettes. Both liked Italian food and mellow rock music. But the first, brief meeting was relatively superficial. "We could hardly talk," Eddy says, "and my dad kept taking pictures. My parents couldn't believe it."

After an hour Bobby and Mike drove back to school. Later that morning Bobby phoned his home and cried, "Dad, Dad, I just met my twin brother!"

Dr. Shafran replied logically, "Bobby, an adoption agency doesn't separate twins." Neither set of parents had been informed that their sons were multiple-birth babies.

That Sunday Bobby and Eddy met again on Long Island and took turns recounting their life experiences. Both have a high I.Q., yet each had had problems in school at the same time. They'd each had psychiatric therapy in 1977 and 1978 and been told their problems were rooted in their adoption; both called that "baloney." They were similarly attracted to older girls—and had serious relationships with women of 27. Their best sport was wrestling, and they had the same favorite moves and fastest pinning time: 18 seconds. "I discovered that whenever I'd had troubles, Eddy had had troubles," Bobby says. "When I had excelled, he'd excelled. It was truly overwhelming."

**That was only the beginning.** The Long Island newspaper *Newsday* heard of the startling reunion about two weeks after it happened and interviewed the twins. The story was picked up by the New York *Post* and the New York *Daily News*.

On the day the article appeared in the *Post*, David Kellman, a 19-year-old college student from Queens, N.Y., saw the picture of Bobby and Eddy. His pulse rate doubled.

"These two people were my mirror image," he says. "But the story didn't give a date of birth, so I tried to keep my emotions low-key and inside till I was sure." That night at home, David hesitantly held out the *Post* and said, "Ma, check this out." Claire Kellman tossed her son a copy of the

*Daily News*—which carried no picture but gave a date of birth—and said, "Check *this* out."

"Right then we knew," David says. "We looked up the phone number of the Galland house. Eddy was out, but his mother answered. I said, 'You're not going to believe this, Mrs. Galland, but my name is David Kellman, and I think I'm the third.'"

That evening David and his parents drove over to the Galland home. Eddy watched as the Kellman car parked beside the curb and "still another me climbed out and started up the walk. I opened the door a little, then closed it. I opened it again, saw his face and closed it again. It was like a double take, a triple take—and the third time I opened it David was saying, in a voice just

> ## "I discovered that whenever I'd had troubles, Eddy had had troubles. When I had excelled, he'd excelled. It was truly overwhelming."

like my own, 'I haven't seen you in 19 years—don't slam the door in my face!'"

Slowly, they moved toward each other. "I can't *believe* this!" they said simultaneously. Then, again in unison, "I can't believe you *said* that!"—and fell into each other's arms.

David pulled out his cigarettes—the same brand Bobby and Eddy smoked. Like his brothers, David had flunked math despite a high I.Q.; had gone through psychiatric care; enjoyed Italian food, wrestling, older women ("not in that order"); and had dreamed he had a brother who looked like him.

David felt "euphoria," and Eddy thoroughly enjoyed the night. "We just kept talking and saying, 'Wow, did you do that, too?'"

**It was probably the first time in history** that identical triplets separated in infancy had been reunited. Each child was brought up in a somewhat different environment by working parents. The Shafrans are medical and legal professionals; Richard and Claire Kellman operate a wholesale housewares business; Elliott Galland is an industrial-arts teacher and his wife, Annette, is an executive secretary.

Predictably, scientists have now flooded the families with requests to study the triplets. But the 19-year-olds are too consumed with their joyful, sometimes zany, self-discovery to hold still for inquiry. "We have never been genuinely, intrinsically happy like this before," explains David. "Give us a chance."

The families' first priority was to contact the adoption agency and inquire why the boys had been separated. None of the parents was pleased with the explanation that, 19 years ago, little was known of the potentially harmful effects of splitting up multiple-birth children. The triplets were said to be the last such infants separated.

No one can be certain whether they would have led less complex emotional lives if they had stayed together, but the presumption is strong. "We all had periods of being miserable, a lot of emotional pain, in spite of having terrific parents," says Bobby. "Psychiatrists told each of us there was some kind of emotional block."

It is a rare, serious moment in an interview with Bobby, David and Eddy. Their eccentric sense of humor seems to combine the drollery of the early Beatles and the horseplay of the Marx Brothers. They often yelp with laughter, then switch gears to calm, straight-faced conversation that invariably ends in one triplet finishing another's sentence. They confess they can be "really wild sometimes" when together, but they're trying, gradually, to settle down.

David intends to become a businessman. Bobby, whose mother says he has been cooking since the age of four, plans to operate hotels and restaurants. Eddy will be a doctor. They phone or see one another half a dozen times a day and meet often at one another's homes.

"They're all so happy," says Dr. Shafran with a smile. "But they're rushing to make up for 19 years of being apart. They get kind of fractious. I only hope they won't let all this distract them from their education and goals. You can't make a career out of being a triplet."

In spite of the wonder of finding "our own flesh and blood," the triplets say they have no interest in locating their biological parents. "There may be an underlying curiosity, but it isn't relevant," Eddy says.

Bobby adds, "A woman gave birth to us. We appreciate that. She made sure we got into good homes, and we appreciate that. But we all have intelligent parents who cared for us, went through trials and heartaches with us. They are our real parents."

All three of the triplets agree with that. ∎

# Now It's Our Turn

In this article for the *Digest*, the President recalled inspiring acts of kindness—and urged everyone to help the less fortunate.

## By Ronald Reagan

In Washington, D.C., two years ago, DeLois Ruffing was down on her luck. She was a certified nurse's aide, but hadn't been able to find a job. In the home she ran for the elderly, some of the residents owed her almost a year's back rent. Her house was in disrepair. The ceiling was falling down around her, and she had no funds to fix the place.

Then three strangers appeared at her door and asked if Ruffing wanted to participate in a program called Christmas in April. They had gotten her name from an inner-city church when they offered to help needy people in the area. If she agreed, volunteers would show up at her home on Saturday, April 30, to repair the ceiling, fix the plumbing, paint the walls and haul away the trash. And they wouldn't charge her a dime.

Ruffing thought that would be marvelous, although she didn't really expect it to happen. Strangers just don't volunteer to help poor people. But on Friday, April 29, two officials of the Washington Building and Construction Trades Council (AFL-CIO) arrived with supplies. They would return in the morning to start work, they said, and bring a dozen other volunteers.

At 8 a.m., the renovation began. In Ruffing's home, as well as in the homes of 17 other residents of the Mt. Pleasant section of Washington, 350 Christmas in April volunteers—attorneys, accountants, journalists, students, housewives, even a judge—swung into action.

Ten hours later—the ceiling and plumbing fixed, walls gleaming—a grateful Ruffing could hardly contain her joy. "I've had *two* Christmases today," she said, with tears in her eyes. "The first was when you people arrived. The second was a call from a temporary-nursing service offering me a job. Next year, if you need help, just let me know."

Program officials took DeLois Ruffing at her word. In 1984, they asked her to serve on the organization's board of directors. Ruffing accepted and soon was busy recruiting other volunteers and appealing for funds; she even cooked 200 pieces of chicken to help celebrate the renovation of 40 homes. "Volunteers helped me when I was down," Ruffing says simply. "Now it's my turn."

*Now it's my turn.* That could be the motto of America's volunteers, for I hear it everywhere I go. All across this great land, millions of citizens contribute time, effort and funds to help the less fortunate.

In Northfield, Minn., for example, a legal secretary decided to aid the poor by sewing and donating clothes. Today Verona Deveney's volunteer effort—called HOPE, for "Help Other People Everywhere"—distributes clothing to 5,000 families a year.

In Philadelphia, 35 dedicated volunteers formed a group called Wheels, which uses nine cars and five vans to transport the sick or handicapped to and from doctors' offices and hospitals. There is never a charge or any reliance on government funds. Since its inception in 1959, Wheels has made more than a million trips.

In Los Angeles, cardiologist James A. Mays began the "Adopt-a-Family Endowment" to encourage black professionals to be role models and help families in need. Fifty families have been "adopted" so far. The result of one recent adoption: two sisters, both of whom dropped out of high school when they became pregnant, returned to earn their diplomas. One has a four-year college scholarship and wants to be an electrical engineer. The other is hoping to become a nurse.

Behind these stories lie some staggering statistics. According to a Gallup Poll, 92 million of us—or 55 percent of the adult population—volunteer our time. Most of the volunteers are familiar actors and actresses on the stage of our daily existence: housewives who take food to shut-ins, teacher's aides, volunteer firefighters who risk their lives to answer every call. Why do they do it? Is our willingness to help people something distinctly American?

One hundred fifty years ago, a young Frenchman, Alexis de Tocqueville, traveled through our country and concluded that the answer is yes. Americans are the most peculiar people in the world, he wrote. If some need develops in a community, a citizen discusses it with his neighbor. Then a committee begins functioning. Soon the problem is solved. All this, he pointed out, is without reference to any bureaucrat. Private citizens do it on their own initiative.

This spirit of voluntarism, then, flows like a deep and mighty river through the history of our nation. Americans have always extended their hands in gestures of assistance. They helped build a neighbor's barn when it burned down and then formed a volunteer fire department so it wouldn't burn again. They harvested the next fellow's crops when he was ill and raised school funds at quilting bees and church socials. In the aftermath of earthquakes and floods, Americans were there. They just took it for granted that neighbor would help neighbor.

But after World War II, the level of that river of voluntarism receded. As government expanded, we abdicated to it tasks that used to be done by the community and the neighborhood. "Why should I get involved?" people asked. "Let the government handle it."

But it was our business all along, and no one realized this more than President John F. Kennedy. "Only by doing the work ourselves," he reminded us, "by giving generously out of our own pockets, can we hope to maintain the authority of the people over the state, to ensure that the people remain the master, the state the servant. Every time we try to lift a problem from our own shoulders and shift it to the government, to the same extent we are sacrificing the liberties of our people."

There is a legitimate role for government. But we mustn't forget: The real source of our progress as a nation is the private sector, which offers more creative and more efficient alternatives to solving our social problems. I'm not advocating private initiatives and volunteer activities as a replacement for budget cuts. I'm advocating them because they're right in their own regard. They're part of what we can proudly call "the American personality."

In 1982, the unemployment rate in eastern Iowa stood above ten percent. That April, at KGAN-TV in Cedar Rapids, news director Bob Jackson came up with an idea. The station had recently aired a report about a man who had been out of work and within minutes an employer had called to offer him a job. Jackson asked, "Why can't we put people back to work with a job-a-thon?"

Station executives agreed to try and scheduled the effort for July 9. Working with Job Service of Iowa, they obtained employer pledges of 319 jobs. Merchants National Bank said it would help underwrite the costs of the three-and-one-half-hour show; unemployed Iowans were invited to appear on camera and discuss the types of jobs they were trying to find.

When I heard what KGAN-TV was doing, I was so touched that I phoned congratulations from Washington. Program host Barry Norris told me that the results were marvelous—applicants had snapped up all 319 jobs—and response was so great that the station repeated its job-a-thon the following year, with equal success.

In 1980, shortly after Los Angeles was selected to host the 1984 Olympic Games, officials began planning to spruce up the town. But they didn't know how to solve one problem—smog. Because trees improve air quality—a million trees would filter 200 tons of particulates from the atmosphere every day—they decided that planting 1 million trees was the way to go. But it would take 20 years and cost $200 million. And that did not include another $200 million needed for maintenance. The city didn't have the funds.

In desperation, officials turned to Andy Lipkis, the 26-year-old founder of a volunteer environmental group called TreePeople. He would see to the planting of all 1 million trees, Lipkis said, and—by involving the entire community—do the job for less than $1 million. Furthermore, he proposed to finish the project *before* the Olympics began!

Few people thought that Lipkis could succeed. But he was undeterred. "We wanted to challenge the people of Los Angeles with an almost impossible task," he says. "Miracles can be accomplished when people join together."

And people *did* join together. A nursery in Pomona asked Lipkis if he "could use" 100,000 trees. And General Telephone Co. of California agreed to underwrite the planting of 250,000 trees. Additionally, the company sent 600 active and retired employees into 300 area schools and recruited more than 70,000 kids to plant the trees.

Last July 23—just five days before the Olympics began—Lipkis received word that the millionth tree was in the ground. Los Angeles had achieved its impossible goal.

After the event, 11-year-old Peter Lin wrote TreePeople and GTE to thank them for the opportunity to participate. "My tree is growing well and strong," he began. "I hope that

# If a neighbor's barn burned, Americans helped rebuild, then formed a volunteer fire department so it wouldn't burn again.

someday I can say I planted the tall, strong tree and feel proud of it."

Well, Peter, you don't have to wait. You can feel proud now.

And so can the millions of others whose unselfish activities have improved the quality of life for the rest of us in so many meaningful ways:

Bill and Pat Barton of Naples, Fla., who helped educate their community about the hazards of drug abuse. Robert Macauley, a businessman in New Canaan, Conn., whose Americares Foundation flies medicines and pharmaceutical supplies to the sick and indigent around the world. The people at ARCO Oil and Gas Co., who pioneered the adopt-a-school program in Dallas and committed themselves to bettering the quality of education there by providing tutoring, guidance and student internships. And Brothers Redevelopment, Inc., in Denver, which helps families buy and rehabilitate homes.

I am confident that the character and generosity of our people will never erode. The mighty river of American voluntarism is rising once again—ensuring our inner strength for generations to come. ∎

# A Last Chance FOR Troubled Boys

*By Lawrence Elliott*

On his ranch with foster sons, Tom Potter shows them what it means to be a man.

PHOTOGRAPHS BY DAN LAMONT

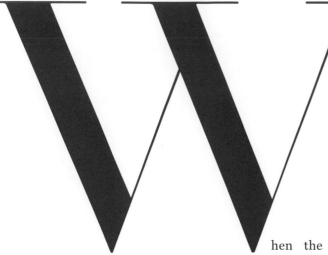

When the car stopped in front of a weathered ranch house, child-service caseworker Laurel Anderson got out first. "You're going to like the Potters," she told the boy with her. Mark Bissonette, Jr., looked around at the mountains rising up out of Oregon's Willamette Valley. He seemed dubious.

Inside, Tom and Maryann Potter greeted them warmly, and Anderson left. Walking to her car, she beseeched the surrounding silence, "Please let this work—we have nowhere else to turn."

Not yet in the sixth grade, Mark was a handful. His mother could no longer control him. Mark's father, who divorced his mother six years earlier, was not in regular contact with him. Mark lied, vandalized his school and stole from his classmates. Diagnosed with attention deficit disorder, he talked compulsively, denying or justifying or gloating about what he had done. Often he lashed out with his fists. He had already been turned out of two foster homes.

That was why he was brought to the Potters'. They have been making a home for boys no one else wants—boys who are down to their last chance, among the toughest cases of the Lane County branch of the State Office for Services to Children and Families. Maryann has a heart that can't say no, and Tom, a rock-solid rancher, teaches the boys how to saddle and ride a horse, rope a steer and hunt for food. He also tells them the hardest truth of all: "In the end only one person in this world can drag you down or lift you up, and that person is you."

Two troubled boys were already living there the summer evening Laurel Anderson dropped Mark off, plus two of the Potters' own kids, Scotty and Jennifer. "We're all one family here," Tom told Mark. "We stand or fall together. You think you want to come live here?"

"What do I gotta do?" Mark asked suspiciously.

"Love us. The way we'll love you. The way families do."

Mark smirked. "What do I *really* gotta do?"

Tom Potter hooked a forefinger inside the boy's shirt and pulled him face to face. "I already told you. Love. Do you know how to love?"

The boy shook his head no.

"Well, the first thing is, you quit making a life out of feeling sorry for yourself. Love is a two-way street. You want it? You have to give it."

Tom then offered Mark what he calls the 30-day deal. Mark could move in with the right to call it quits any time before one month passed, no arguments. "After that," said

Tom, "we're stuck with each other. If you do wrong, I'll punish you. If you run away, I'll come after you. Because then you'll be part of the family, see? And families stick together."

Mark agreed. No one was betting he would stick it out.

The Potters didn't start out to be foster parents. After a tour in Vietnam, Tom became a police officer, then tried several other jobs before deciding to raise livestock full time. Soon after he married Maryann, a health-care customer-service representative, he settled down to run cattle and horses on mostly leased land around Eugene.

Then one day Maryann was touched by a newspaper article on foster care. "Everybody wants babies," she told Tom. "But the older kids are falling between the cracks." The two decided to become foster parents. Soon the first of many foster sons came into their home.

He could have been the last. Wes Alford, a husky 17-year-old, was a chronic runaway, experimented with drugs and was on probation. Tom devoted a lot of time talking to Wes and thought he was making progress. But one evening, irritated at something, Wes told Maryann to shut up and pushed past her.

The next thing he knew, he had been flung on the couch and Tom, breathing fire, was standing over him. "Listen to me, son," Tom said. "As long as you're in this house, Maryann Potter is your mother. Now get up and apologize."

"I won't," came the choked reply. "And I am going to tell my caseworker that you physically abused me."

"Okay. Let's do it right now." Tom grabbed Wes by the collar and yanked him to the phone. "Tell him you'll be on his doorstep in 15 minutes!"

Twelve years later, recalling that crucial instant in his life, Wes said, "We stood there eyeballing each other really hard. My first reaction was to fight Tom. But then I suddenly realized that I couldn't keep pushing my way around."

He begged Maryann's forgiveness, and she took him in her arms. He struggled to speak and finally said, "Thanks for saving me."

Little by little, Wes began to work out a new identity. Now married and holding a steady job, he gave Tom's name to his first son. "Without the Potters' influence, I don't know where I'd be today," Wes says.

Would Tom really have thrown him out 13 years ago? "Let's just say it was important for him to believe I would," Tom replies.

On a summer morning in 1989, Tom went to wake his own son Scotty and found one of Scotty's friends, Robbie Williamson, in the second bunk.

He had argued with his father again, Robbie said in a rush. He was never going back home. Never.

"Let's have some breakfast," Tom replied. "Then we'll sort this out."

Robbie stayed on. Tom made sure that it was all right with his mother, and he made sure that Robbie went to see her regularly. The Potters treated him as their own but didn't let him forget he had parents in town. And six years later, when he was 19, Robbie made peace with his father and went home.

> ## "Deep inside these boys is a spark of humanity. If you reach it and feed it— well, then, maybe you have a chance to help a lost boy."

Robbie's arrival was a turning point. The Potters decided that if they had room for him, they could take in even more than the one or two foster boys they'd been raising at a time.

**Mark's first 30 days, in the summer of 1988,** were turbulent. He stole $20 from Maryann and deliberately dropped a stack of plates. Learning to ride, he spurred his horse hard enough to draw blood. For these transgressions he spent a lot of time cleaning horse stalls and hauling rocks and stacking them into piles.

But he yelped with glee at the cowboy boots Maryann bought him, and he started calling her and Tom Mom and Dad, the way the other kids did. And when school opened, he asked if he could register as Mark Potter. "You staying?" Tom asked.

"If you want me to," Mark replied.

Tom stuck out his hand. "Put 'er there, Mark Potter."

Still, it was never clear that Mark would make it. Tom had to tell him everything twice, and even then he didn't seem to get it. "Never forget to check the cinch, or the saddle will slide." Oblivious, Mark would put his foot in the stirrup and sure enough, the saddle would roll underneath the horse, and Mark would end up on the ground.

him once, "you want to spend your life pumping gas or picking trash off the side of the road? Because that's all you've got to look forward to without a high-school diploma."

"I'm doing the best I can," the boy sullenly replied.

"I don't think so. I've seen you at your best. And that's a lot better than D's."

That would pump the boy up for a while. But inevitably his attention would drift. Yet Mark did care. He desperately wanted to be as good as the other boys, only he didn't want anyone to know how hard he was trying.

Sometimes the fury simmering within would erupt. One night when Mark was 16, one of the others teased him about his struggle with homework. As Mark started after his tormentor, Tom grabbed him in mid-flight. "Whoa there, boy! Hold on to your cool."

"Did you hear what he said?" Mark shrieked.

"I did, and that was wrong," Tom said. "But bashing in your brother's head over it would be worse."

"Yeah, that's always the way. You're always sticking up for them!" Mark yelled. "You never fooled me with all that hot air about families and loving. Maybe you loved them guys, but you never loved me." Then he ran to his room and slammed the door.

In the middle of the night, Scotty woke his parents to say Mark was gone. Tom got in the pickup and headed toward Eugene. About 30 minutes later Mark's forlorn figure rose up in the headlights. "Get in," Tom said. Mark knew enough not to argue. "What're you planning to do?" Tom asked.

"Get a job."

"You've got a job. You're working on a high-school diploma, remember? You think your mother and I don't know how hard it's been for you? And now that you're almost there, you want to dump it all and become another bum? America doesn't need another bum, Mark."

"Ah, what do you care?"

They drove on in silence. Finally Tom said he would take him wherever he wanted to go.

"I want to go home," said Mark.

"Didn't I tell you?"

"Ah, who the hell cares?" Mark would respond. That would cost him two hours of packing manure from the barn to the far corners of the field, because Tom did not tolerate disrespect. But it didn't cure Mark.

"Watch your horse's ears," he'd tell the boys while trail riding. "They telegraph what she's going to do next. If she pins them back, it could mean trouble."

But when Tom looked around at Mark, he saw only glazed eyes or a perpetual-motion mouth.

Nor could Tom and Maryann keep him focused on school. As the years went by, Mark was constantly in remedial classes yet still got D's and F's. "Listen," Tom said to

**Nothing much changed.** He still talked incessantly and blew up. But slowly his grades improved, and as a reward, Tom took him along on a trail-riding party with two Eastern businessmen.

Mark attached himself to them, his mouth going its customary hundred miles an hour. When they made camp the first night, Tom apologized. "He's a terrific kid," he said, "but you just can't shut him up. I hope he's not spoiling things."

"Are you kidding?" one of the men replied. "I just hope we can remember everything he taught us." And then, imitating Mark's sing-song, he started reciting the day's lessons: "Never forget to check the cinch, or the saddle will slide. Watch your horse's ears."

Tom gasped. It sounded like a tape recording of things he'd tried to teach Mark. Later he threw an arm around the boy's shoulders and joked, "So tell me, son—as an outsider, what do you think of the human race?"

Mark said with a grin, "Aw, Dad." And they hugged.

In the winter of 1996, in the middle of his junior year, Mark turned 18 and by Oregon law was emancipated—free to decide his own future. He decided to live with his natural mother, who had her life together.

"Don't you worry, Dad," Mark reassured Tom. "I am gonna get that diploma and apply all that good stuff you taught me about believing in myself. You'll see—it's gonna work."

Tom smiled and pulled him close. His heart was heavy, but he felt pride, too. He and Maryann had lent a hand to a confused youngster who now seemed sure of what he had to do. It was his moment of manhood.

Last June came the call Tom and Maryann Potter had hoped for. Mark had earned his high-school diploma.

# Tom teaches them how to ride. And tells them, "Only one person in this world can drag you down or lift you up, and that person is you."

The Potters now have two boys and expect to take in two more soon. The youngsters are learning to train horses and raise livestock, gaining skills and self-confidence along the way. And, once again, the Potters are helping their cowboys reach manhood.

"Deep inside these boys is a spark of humanity. That's God-given. If you reach it and feed it—well, then maybe you have a chance to help a lost boy," Tom says.

"Is there anything more rewarding than investing your heart and hopes in a kid and seeing him succeed?" he asks. ■

## HUMOR **IN UNIFORM**

**MY WIFE,** Anita, worked at the Navy exchange dry cleaners while I was stationed at the submarine base in Groton, Conn.

One evening a familiar-looking man in civilian clothes came to pick up his dry cleaning. Anita was sure he was on my crew and that she had met him at the "Welcome Aboard" family briefing a few weeks earlier.

As she handed him his change, she said, "Excuse me, but aren't you on my husband's boat?"

"No, ma'am," my commanding officer replied, "I believe your husband is on my boat."

-MICHAEL GORIUP

**ONE NIGHT** at McChord Air Force Base in Washington, I was dispatched to check out the security fence where an alarm had gone off. The fence was at the end of the base runway. When I got to the scene, I found that a raccoon was the culprit, so I ran around and flapped my arms to scare off the animal.

Suddenly an air-traffic controller came over the public-address system and announced loudly, "Attention to the airman at the end of the runway. You are cleared for takeoff."

-CHAD BLAKE

**I WAS LOADING** our aircraft carrier with supplies when an ensign saw one of my friends spit on the hangar floor, which was already covered with oil and refuse. The officer was appalled. "Sailor," he demanded, "would you spit on your floor at home?"

"No, sir," my friend replied. "But I wouldn't land airplanes on my roof either."

-MICKEY HOMAN

Did a chance meeting, after a change of routine, give two strangers the opportunity of their lives, or was it divine intervention?

# It Happened On The Brooklyn SUBWAY

## By Paul Deutschman

There are two explanations for what happened as the result of the subway ride taken by Hungarian-born Marcel Sternberger on the afternoon of January 10, 1948.

Some people will say that Sternberger's sudden impulse to visit a sick friend in Brooklyn—and the bright world of dramatic events that followed—was part of a string of lucky coincidences. Others will see the guiding hand of Divine Providence in everything that happened that day.

Whatever the explanation, here are the facts:

Sternberger, a New York portrait photographer living in a Long Island suburb, had followed for years an unchanging routine in going from his home to his office on Fifth Avenue. A methodical man of nearly 50, with bushy white hair, guileless brown eyes and the bouncing enthusiasm of a czardas dancer of his native Hungary, Sternberger always

took the 9:09 Long Island Railroad train to Woodside, where he caught a subway to the city.

On the morning of January 10, he boarded the 9:09 as usual. En route he suddenly decided to visit Laszlo Victor, a Hungarian friend who lived in Brooklyn and who was ill.

"I don't know why I decided to go to see him that morning," Sternberger told me some weeks afterward. "I could have done it after office hours. But I kept thinking that he could stand a little cheering up."

Accordingly, at Ozone Park Sternberger changed to the subway for Brooklyn, went to his friend's house and stayed until mid-afternoon. He then boarded a Manhattan-bound subway for his office.

"The car was crowded," Sternberger told me, "and there seemed to be no chance of a seat. But just as I entered, a man sitting by the door suddenly jumped up to leave and I slipped into the empty place.

"I've been living in New York long enough not to start conversations with strangers. But, being a photographer, I have the peculiar habit of analyzing people's faces, and I was struck by the features of the passenger to my left. He was probably in his late 30s, and his eyes seemed to have a hurt expression in them. He was reading a Hungarian-language newspaper, and something prompted me to turn to him and say in Hungarian, 'I hope you don't mind if I glance at your paper.'

"The man seemed surprised to be addressed in his native language, but he answered politely, 'You may read it now. I'll have time later on.'

"During the half-hour ride to town we had quite a conversation. He said his name was Paskin. A law student when the war started, he had been put into a labor battalion and sent to the Ukraine. Later he was captured by the Russians and put to work burying the German dead. After the war he had covered hundreds of miles on foot, until he reached his home in Debrecen, a large city in eastern Hungary.

"I myself knew Debrecen quite well, and we talked about it for a while. Then he told me the rest of his story. When he went to the apartment once occupied by his father, mother, brothers and sisters, he found strangers living there. Then he went upstairs to the apartment he and his wife had once had. It also was occupied by strangers. None of them had ever heard of his family.

"As he was leaving, full of sadness, a boy ran after him, calling, '*Paskin bacsi! Paskin bacsi!*' That means 'Uncle Paskin.' The child was the son of some old neighbors of his. He went to the boy's home and talked to his parents. 'Your whole family is dead,' they told him. 'The Nazis took them and your wife to Auschwitz.'

"Auschwitz was one of the worst concentration camps. Paskin thought of the Nazi gas chambers and gave up all hope. A few days later, too heartsick to remain longer in Hungary, which to him was a funeral land, he set out again on foot, stealing across border after border until he reached Paris. He had managed to emigrate to the United States in October 1947, just three months before I met him.

"All the time he had been talking, I kept thinking that somehow his story seemed familiar. Suddenly I knew why. A young woman whom I had met recently at the home of friends had also been from Debrecen; she had been sent to Auschwitz; from there she had been transferred to work in a German munitions factory. Her relatives had been killed in the gas chambers. Later she was liberated by the

> "Paskin thought of the Nazi gas chambers and gave up all hope. A few days later, too heartsick to remain in a funeral land, he set out on foot."

Americans and brought here in the first boatload of Displaced Persons in 1946. Her story had moved me so much that I had written down her address and phone number, intending to invite her to meet my family and thus help relieve the terrible emptiness of her present life.

"It seemed impossible that there could be any connection between these two people. But when I reached my station, I stayed on the train and asked in what I hoped was a casual voice, 'Is your first name Bela?'

"He turned pale. 'Yes!' he answered. 'How did you know?'

"I fumbled anxiously in my address book. 'Was your wife's name Marya?'

"He looked as if he were about to faint. 'Yes! Yes!' he said.

"I said, 'Let's get off the train.' I took him by the arm at the next station and led him to a phone booth. He stood there like a man in a trance while I searched for the number in my address book. It seemed hours before I had the woman called Marya Paskin on the other end. (Later I learned her room was alongside the telephone, but she was in the habit of never answering it because she had so few friends and the calls were always for someone else. This time, however, there was no one else at home, and after letting it ring for a while, she answered it.)

"When I heard her voice at last, I told her who I was and asked her to describe her husband. She seemed surprised at the question, but gave me a description. Then I asked her where she had lived in Debrecen, and she told me the address.

"Asking her to hold the wire, I turned to Paskin and said, 'Did you and your wife live on such-and-such a street?'

"'Yes!' Bela exclaimed. He was white as a sheet and trembling.

"'Try to be calm,' I urged him. 'Something miraculous is about to happen to you. Here, take this telephone and talk to your wife!'

"He nodded his head in mute bewilderment, his eyes bright with tears. He took the receiver, listened a moment to his wife's voice, then suddenly cried, 'This is Bela! This is Bela!' and began to mumble hysterically. Seeing that the poor fellow was so excited he couldn't talk coherently, I took the receiver from his shaking hands.

"I began talking to Marya, who also sounded hysterical. 'Stay where you are,' I told her. 'I am sending your husband to you. He will be there in a few minutes.'

"Bela was crying like a baby and saying over and over again, 'It is my wife. I go to my wife!'

"At first I thought I had better accompany Paskin, lest the man should faint from excitement, but decided that this was a moment in which no strangers should intrude. Putting Paskin into a taxicab, I directed the driver to take him to Marya's address, paid the fare and said goodbye."

Bela Paskin's reunion with his wife was a moment so poignant, so electric with suddenly released emotion, that afterward neither he nor Marya could recall much about it.

"I remember only that when I left the phone I walked to the mirror like in a dream to see maybe if my hair had turned gray," she said later. "The next thing I know, a taxi stops in front of the house, and it is my husband who comes toward me. Details I cannot remember; only this I know— that I was happy for the first time in many years.

"Even now it is difficult to believe that it happened. We have both suffered so much; I have almost lost the capability to be not afraid. Each time my husband goes from the house, I say to myself, 'Will anything happen to take him from me again?'"

Her husband is confident that no horrible misfortune will ever again befall them. "Providence has brought us together," he says simply. "It was meant to be."

Skeptical persons would no doubt attribute the events of that memorable afternoon to mere chance. But was it chance that made Sternberger suddenly decide to visit his sick friend, and hence take a subway line that he had never ridden before? Was it chance that caused the man sitting by the door of the car to rush out just as Sternberger came in? Was it chance that caused Bela Paskin to be sitting beside Sternberger reading a Hungarian newspaper?

Was it chance—or did God ride the Brooklyn subway that afternoon? ∎

## LAUGHTER, THE BEST MEDICINE

**LOU SEES A SIGN** in front of a house: "Talking Dog for Sale." Intrigued, he rings the bell and the owner shows him the dog.

"What's your story?" Lou asks.

The dog says, "I discovered I had this gift when I was just a pup. The CIA signed me up, and soon I was jetting around the world, sitting at the feet of spies and world leaders, gathering important information and sending it back home. When I tired of that lifestyle, I joined the FBI, where I helped catch drug lords and gunrunners. I was wounded in the line of duty, received some medals and now a movie is being made of my life."

"How much do you want for the dog?" Lou asks the owner.

"Ten dollars," says the owner.

Lou is incredulous. "Why on earth would you sell that remarkable dog for so little?"

"Because he's a liar. He didn't do any of that stuff."

**ADAM RETURNED HOME** late one night, and Eve confronted him at the door.

"You're seeing another woman, aren't you?" she accused.

"Don't be silly," he replied. "You're the only woman on earth."

Later, while half-asleep, Adam felt a tickle on his chest. "What are you doing?" he asked Eve.

"Counting your ribs."

This man says to the psychiatrist, "Doc, every time I get into bed, I think there's somebody under it. You have to help me."

"Come to me three times a week for two years, and I'll cure your fears," the psychiatrist says. "And I'll only charge you $200 a visit."

"I'll think about it," the man says.

Six months later, the psychiatrist meets the man on the street. The psychiatrist asks why the man never came back.

"For $200 a visit? A bartender cured me for ten."

"Is that so? How?"

"He told me to cut the legs off the bed."

# Which Was 'The Real Linda'?

By J. Anthony Lukas

The mystery of her final days was deepened by a dual identity. Was she the Linda of Greenwich, Conn., or of Greenwich Village?

The windows of Dr. Irving Sklar's reception room at 2 Fifth Avenue, New York City, look out across Washington Square—from it a patient can watch pigeons circling Stanford White's dignified Washington Arch, children playing hopscotch on the square's wide walkways. Dr. Sklar has long been the family dentist of the Irving Fitzpatricks, who live in a 30-room home a mile from the

ILLUSTRATION BY DAVID M. BRINLEY

Greenwich, Conn., Country Club, and for them "the Village" has always been the Henry James scene they saw out Sklar's windows. But for their 18-year-old-daughter, Linda—at least in the last ten weeks of her life—the Village was a different scene whose ingredients included crash pads, acid trips, freaking out, witches and warlocks.

If the Fitzpatricks' knowledge of the Village stopped at Washington Square, their knowledge of their daughter stopped at the unsettling but familiar image of a young, talented girl overly impatient to taste the joys of life. Reality in both cases went far beyond. In mid-October, a week after Linda's murder, the Fitzpatricks were still unable to believe what their daughter had gone through in her last days.

Which was "the real Linda"—the Linda of Greenwich, Conn., or the Linda of Greenwich Village? As the New York *Times* investigated, it found her a mixture so tangled that Linda herself probably did not know.

The forces at work on young people like Linda are the source of puzzlement for many other parents and of studies by social workers and psychologists. Until a few months ago, Linda—or "Fitzpoo," as she was known to family and friends—seemed a happy product of wealthy American suburbia. "Linda is a well-rounded, fine, healthy girl," her mother, a well-groomed woman in a high-collared chocolate-brown dress, said during the three-hour *Times* interview in which she often used the present tense in talking of her daughter.

> ## "She had lots of men up there all the time. Anybody off the street—the dirtiest hippies she could find."

Born in Greenwich, Linda attended Greenwich Country Day School, where she excelled in field hockey, swimming and riding. She went on to Oldfields, a four-year college-preparatory school in Glencoe, Md. A blonde tending to pudginess, she never quite matched the striking good looks of her mother or her elder sister Cindy. At country-club dances she often sat in the corner and talked with one of her half brothers; but, apparently more interested in sports and painting than dancing, she never seemed to mind much.

Last June Linda returned from Oldfields, and after several weeks in Greenwich, she left with the family for a month

in Bermuda. "We always do things as a family," said Irving Fitzpatrick, a tall, athletic-looking, wealthy spice importer.

The family included seven children: Linda and 9-year-old Melissa (Missy) from this marriage; Perry, 32, Robert, 30, Carol, 27, and David, 25, from Fitzpatrick's previous marriage, which ended in divorce; and Cindy from Mrs. Fitzpatrick's first marriage, which also ended in divorce. But this time only Linda and Missy accompanied their parents to Bermuda, while Cindy and her husband joined them later for ten days.

As the Fitzpatricks remember it, Linda spent "a typical Bermuda vacation": swimming in the ocean, beach parties, hours of painting, occasional shopping expeditions to town.

On July 31, the family returned to Greenwich, where Linda spent most of August. Again, the family insists she was "the girl we knew and loved." They say she spent most of her time painting in the studio in the back of the house. But she found plenty of time for swimming with friends in the large robin's-egg-blue pool. If Linda went to New York during August, it was "just a quick trip in and out—just for the day."

**Linda's friends in the Village have a different story** of her summer.

"Linda told me she took LSD and smoked grass [marijuana] many times during her stay in Bermuda," recalled Susan Robinson, a small, shy hippie who ran away last May from her home on Cape Cod, Mass. "She talked a lot about a fellow who gave her a capsule of acid [LSD] down there and how she was going to send him one."

The two-room apartment of Susan and her husband, David, served last summer as a "crash pad"—a place where homeless hippies could spend the night. "Linda first showed up one evening early in August with a guy named Pigeon," Susan said. "She'd just bought Pigeon some acid. She stayed maybe a couple of hours and then took off.

"A few nights later she came back with a kid from Boston. She turned him on, too [gave him some LSD]. She was always doing that. She'd come into the city on weekends with $30 or $40 and would buy acid for people who needed some."

David Robinson, a gentle, black-bearded young man who worked in a brassiere factory, recalled how Linda turned him on, on August 22. "We went to this guy who sold us three capsules for $10 apiece," he said. "She put one away to send to the guy in Bermuda, gave me one and took one herself. We were out in Tompkins Park, and we dropped it [swallowed it] right there. Around midnight we walked over to Cooper Union Square, where we had a very good discussion with a drunk. By then we were really flying. She was very, very groovy. At

8 a.m. Linda took the subway up to Grand Central and got on the train to Greenwich. She must still have been flying when she got home."

**That weekend Mrs. Fitzpatrick was getting Linda** ready for school. "We bought her almost an entire new wardrobe," she recalled, "and Linda even agreed to get her hair cut."

For months Fitzpatrick had complained about Linda's hair, which flowed down over her shoulders, but Linda didn't want to change it. Then at the end of August she agreed. "We went to Saks Fifth Avenue and the hairdresser gave her a blunt cut, short and full. She looked so cute and smart. Hardly a hippie thing to do."

The first day of school was only 11 days off when Linda went to New York on September 1. The next day she told her mother she didn't want to go back to Oldfields—she wanted to live and paint in the Village. "We couldn't have been more surprised," Mrs. Fitzpatrick said.

"We talked about it all through the weekend," Fitzpatrick added. "Finally, on Sunday night we gave her our reluctant permission, though not our approval."

"After all," her mother said, "Linda's whole life was art. She had a burning desire to be something in the art world. I knew how she felt. I wanted to be a dancer or an artist when I was young, too.

"Linda told us that she was going to live at the Village Plaza, a very nice hotel on Washington Place, near the university. 'I'll be perfectly safe, Mother,' she kept saying. 'It's a perfectly nice place, with a doorman.' She said she'd be rooming with a girl named Paula Bush, a 22-year-old receptionist from a good family. That made us feel a lot better."

Linda left for New York the next morning. The family never saw her alive again.

**The Village Plaza has no doorman.** The stooped desk clerk said, "Sure, I remember Linda." And riffling through a pile of thumb-marked cards, he came up with one that had Linda's name inked at the top in neat schoolgirl penmanship. Below it in pencil was written: "Paul Bush. Bob Brumberger."

"Yeah," the clerk said. "She moved here on September 4, Labor Day, with these two hippie guys. They had Room 504. She paid the full month's rent—$120—in advance. Of course she had lots of other men up there all the time. Anybody off the street—the dirtiest, bearded hippies she could find.

"I kept telling her she hadn't ought to act like that. She didn't pay me any attention, but she never answered back real snappy like some of the other girls. She had something, I don't know—class. The day she checked out—oh, about

September 20—she said, 'I guess I caused you a lot of trouble,' and I said, 'Oh it wasn't any trouble, really.' You want to see the room?"

The elevator was out of order. The stairs were dark and narrow, heavy with the sweet reek of marijuana. A knock, and the door to 504 swung open. A bearded young man took his place again on the swaybacked double bed that filled half the room. He and three girls were plucking chocolates out of a box. On the mirror above the dresser with one drawer missing was scrawled, "Tea Heads Forever"

> ## "I don't believe Linda had anything to do with hippies. I expressed my abhorrence for them, and her comments were like mine."

[a tea head is a marijuana smoker], and in lighter pencil, "War is Hell." Red plastic flowers hung from an overhead light fixture.

**"Would you like to see Linda's room?"** her mother asked. On the third floor Mrs. Fitzpatrick opened the red curtains in the large room. "Red and white are Linda's favorite colors," Mrs. Fitzpatrick said, taking in the red-and-white-striped wallpaper, the twin beds with red bedspreads, the red pillow with white lettering, "Decisions, Decisions, Decisions."

On the shelves, between the ceramic collie and a glass Bambi, were Edith Hamilton's *The Greek Way* and Agatha Christie's *Murder at Hazelmoor*. Nearby was a stack of records. In the bright bathroom hung ribbons from the Oldfields Horse Show and the Greenwich Riding Association Show. "As you can see, she was such a nice, outgoing, happy girl," her mother said. "If anything's changed, it's changed awfully fast."

The Fitzpatricks said they had been reassured about Linda's life in the Village because she said she had a job making posters for a company called Poster Bazaar at $80 a week.

**The records show Linda worked for $2 an hour** selling dresses at a shop called Fred Leighton's Mexican Imports, Ltd. On the third day she was discharged. "She was always coming in late," a salesgirl said.

David Robinson said Linda supported herself from then on by panhandling on Washington Square. "She was pretty good at it," he said. "She always got enough to eat." Yet "she had a thing about money. Once she told me she wanted to get a job with Hallmark Cards drawing those little cartoons. She said she'd make $40,000 a year, rent a big apartment on the Upper East Side and then invite all her hippie friends up there."

**"Linda was very shy," her mother said.** "When a boy got interested in her, she'd almost always lose interest in him. She got a proposal in August from a very nice boy from Arizona. She told me, 'I like him, but he's just too anxious.' The boy sent flowers for the funeral. That was thoughtful."

The Robinsons and Linda's other friends in the Village said there were always men in her life there: first Pigeon, then the boy from Boston, then Paul Bush, who carried a

# Linda said she was a witch: When she wished for money, it "floated down from heaven."

live lizard named Lyndon on a string around his neck. Bush, now in San Francisco, was interviewed by telephone.

"I met Linda at the Robinsons' about August 18—a few days after I got to town," he recalled. "We wandered around together. She said her parents bugged her, always hollered at her. So I said I'd get a pad with her and Brumberger, this kid from New Jersey.

"She said she'd tell her parents she was living with a girl named Paula Bush. That was okay with me. I only stayed a week anyway, and Brumberger even less. Then she brought in some other guy—tall, with long hair and a beard."

This may have been Ed, a tall hippie the Robinsons saw with Linda several times in mid-September. Later came James L. (Groovy) Hutchinson, the man with whom—in less than a month—she would be killed.

Toward the end of September, Susan Robinson said, Linda told her she feared she was pregnant. "She was very

worried about the effect of LSD on the baby, and since I was pregnant too, we talked about it for quite a while."

"I don't believe Linda really had anything to do with the hippies," her father said. "I remember during August we were in this room watching a CBS special about the San Francisco hippies. I expressed my abhorrence for the whole thing, and her comments were like mine. I don't believe she was attracted to them."

**Her friends say Linda was fascinated** by the San Francisco scene. Susan recalled that suddenly on October 1 Linda turned up at her pad and said she had been to Haight-Ashbury. "She said she stayed out there only two days; that it was a really bad scene; that everybody was on speed [a powerful drug called methedrine]. She said she got out and drove back with two warlocks [male witches] she met out there. They could snap their fingers and make light bulbs pop.

"This didn't surprise me," Susan said. "Linda told me several times she was a witch. She discovered this one day sitting on a beach when she wished she had some money, and three dollar bills floated down from heaven."

One of Linda's self-styled warlock friends, who calls himself Pepsi, is in his late 20s, with long, sandy hair, a scruffy beard, heavily tattooed forearms, wire-rim glasses and high suede boots. "My buddy and I ran into Linda in a club in Indianapolis called the Glory Hole," Pepsi said. "You could see right away she was a real meth monster [methedrine user]. We were two days driving back. We got in on October 1, and she put up with me and my buddy in this pad on Avenue B. She was supposed to keep it clean, but all she ever did all day was sit around. She had this real weird imagination, but she was like talking in smaller and smaller circles. She was supposed to be this great artist, but it was just teeny-bopper stuff.

"It sounds like I'm knocking her. I'm not. She was a good kid, if she hadn't been so freaked out on meth. She had a lot of, what do you call it, potential. Sometimes she was a lot of fun to be with. We went out on the Staten Island Ferry one day at dawn and surfing once on Long Island."

Pepsi saw Linda at 10 p.m. on October 8 standing in front of the Cave on Avenue A with Groovy Hutchinson. She said she'd taken a grain and a half of speed and was "high." Three hours later she and Groovy were dead—their nude bodies stretched out on a boiler-room floor, their heads shattered by bricks. The police charged two men with the murders and were continuing their investigation.

"It's too late for the whole thing to do us much good," her brother Perry said after he had been told of her life in the Village. "But maybe somebody else can learn something from it." ■

**SIX GUYS** are playing poker when Smith loses $500 on a single hand, clutches his chest and falls over dead. Who's going to tell his wife? they all wonder. They draw straws, and Anderson picks the short one. They tell him to be discreet and break it to her gently.

"No problem," Anderson says. So he drives over to the Smith house and knocks on the door. The wife answers. "Your husband just lost $500 playing cards," he tells her.

She screams and says, "Tell him to drop dead!"

Anderson replies, "Okay. I'll tell him."

**PHIL WAS DRIVING** down a country road late one night when he felt a big thud. He got out of the car and looked around, but the road was empty. Since there was nothing else to be done, he drove on home.

In the morning the sheriff was standing at his doorstep. "You're under arrest for hitting a pig and leaving the scene," the lawman told him with a frown. "Please come with me."

Phil couldn't believe his ears. "But how could you possibly know that's what happened?" he asked.

"It wasn't hard," the sheriff replied. "The pig squealed."

**"I'VE REALLY HAD IT WITH MY DOG.** He'll chase anyone on a bike."

"So what are you going to do—leave him at the pound? Sell him?"

"No, nothing that drastic. I think I'll just take his bike away."

**STEVIE WONDER** meets Tiger Woods. Stevie mentions that he, too, is a golfer. "When I tee off," the blind musician explains, "I have a guy call to me from the green. My sharp sense of hearing lets me aim."

Tiger is skeptical. When Stevie suggests that they play a round for $100,000, Tiger quickly accepts. He figures it's the easiest money he'll ever make.

"So when do you want to play?"

Stevie shrugs. "Pick any night."

**HOW MANY** "real men" does it take to change a light bulb? None. "Real men" aren't afraid of the dark.

**A COUPLE** of dog owners are arguing about whose dog is smarter.

"My dog is so smart," says the first owner, "that every morning he waits for the paper boy to come around. He tips the kid and then brings the newspaper to me, along with my morning coffee."

"I know," says the second owner.

"How do you know?"

"My dog told me."

**THERE IS A KNOCK** on St. Peter's door. He looks out and a man is standing there. St. Peter is about to begin his interview when the man disappears.

A short time later there's another knock. St. Peter gets the door, sees the same man, opens his mouth to speak, and the man disappears once again.

"Hey, are you playing games with me?" St. Peter calls after him.

"No," the man's distant voice replies anxiously. "They're trying to resuscitate me."

**SOME THINGS** you never want to hear at the tattoo parlor:

- "'Eagle'? I thought you said 'beagle.'"
- "Boy, I hate it when I get hiccups."
- "Hey, buddy, we ran out of red, so I used pink."
- "Two O's in 'Bob,' right?"
- "I bet you can't tell I've never done this before."
- "Anything else you want to say? You've got all kinds of room back here."

# Lincoln Goes to Gettysburg

The President was not known as an orator, and asking him to speak was an afterthought.

*By Carl Sandburg*

ILLUSTRATION BY ROBERTO PARADA

**W**hen Governor Curtin of Pennsylvania set aside November 19, 1863, for the dedication of a National Soldiers' Cemetery at Gettysburg, the only invitation President Lincoln received to attend the ceremonies was a printed circular.

The duties of orator of the day had fallen on Edward Everett. An eminent figure, perhaps the foremost of all American classical orators, he had been governor of Massachusetts, ambassador to Great Britain and president of Harvard. There were four published volumes of his orations. His lectures on Washington, delivered 122 times in three years, had in 1859 brought a fund of $58,000, which he gave for the purchase of Mount Vernon as a permanent shrine.

Serene, suave, handsomely venerable in his sixty-ninth year, Everett was a natural choice of the Pennsylvania commissioners, who gave him two months to prepare his address. The decision to invite Lincoln to speak was an afterthought. As one of the commissioners later wrote, "The question was raised as to his ability to speak upon such a solemn occasion; the invitation was not settled upon until about two weeks before the exercises were held."

In these dark days Lincoln was far from popular in many quarters. Some newspapers claimed that the President was going to make a stump speech over the graves of the Gettysburg dead as a political show. Thaddeus Stevens, Republican floor leader in the House, believed in '63 that Lincoln was a "dead card" in the political deck. He favored Chase for the next President, and hearing that Lincoln and Secretary of State Seward were going to Gettysburg, he commented, "The dead going to bury the dead."

On the day before the ceremony a special train decorated with red-white-and-blue bunting stood ready to take the presidential party to Gettysburg. When his escort remarked that they had no time to lose, Lincoln said he felt like an Illinois man who was going to be hanged, and as the man passed along the road on the way to the gallows, the crowds kept pushing into the way and blocking passage. The condemned man at last called out, "Boys, you needn't be in such a hurry; there won't be any fun till I get there."

Reaching Gettysburg, Lincoln was driven to a private residence on the public square. The sleepy country town was overflowing. Private homes were filled with notables and nondescripts. Hundreds slept on the floors of hotels. Bands blared till late in the night. When serenaders called on the President for a speech, he responded: "In my position it is sometimes important that I should not say foolish things." (A voice: "If you can help it.") "It very often happens that the only way to help it is to say nothing at all. Believing that is my present condition this evening, I must beg of you to excuse me from addressing you further." The crowd didn't feel it was much of a speech. They went next door with the band and blared for Seward.

Beset with problems attendant on the conduct of the war, Lincoln had had little time to prepare his address. About 10 o'clock that night before the ceremony he sat down in his room to do more work on it. It was midnight or later when he went to sleep.

At least 15,000 people were on Cemetery Hill for the exercises the next day when the procession from Gettysburg arrived on foot and on horseback. The President's horse seemed small for him. One of the commissioners, riding just behind the President, noted that he sat erect and looked majestic to begin with, and then got to thinking so his body leaned forward, his arms hung limp and his head bent far down.

The parade had begun to move at 11, and in 15 minutes it was over. But the orator of the day had not arrived.

On the train back to Washington, the President was weary, talked little and had a wet towel across his forehead. "That speech," he said, "was a flat failure."

Bands played till noon. Mr. Everett arrived. On the platform sat state governors, Army officers, foreign ministers, Members of Congress, the President and his party.

When Edward Everett was introduced, he bowed low to Lincoln, then stood in silence before a crowd that stretched to limits that would test his voice. Around were the wheat fields, the meadows, the peach orchards and beyond, the contemplative blue ridge of a low mountain range. He had taken note of these in his prepared and rehearsed address. "Overlooking these broad fields now reposing from the labors of the waning year, the mighty Alleghenies dimly towering before us, the graves of our brethren beneath our feet, it is with hesitation that I raise my poor voice to break the eloquent silence of God and Nature."

He proceeded: "It was appointed by law in Athens,—" and gave an extended sketch of the manner in which the Greeks cared for their dead who fell in battle. He gave an outline of how the war began, traversed decisive features of the three days' battles at Gettysburg, denounced the doctrine of state sovereignty, drew parallels from European history and came to his peroration quoting Pericles on dead patriots: "The whole earth is the sepulcher of illustrious men." He spoke for an hour and 57 minutes. It was the effort of his life and embodied the perfections of the school of oratory in which he had spent his career.

When the time came for Lincoln to speak, he put on his steelbowed glasses, rose and holding in one hand the two sheets of paper at which he occasionally glanced, he delivered the address in his high-pitched and clear-carrying voice. A photographer bustled about with his equipment, but before he had his head under the hood for an exposure, the President had said "by the people and for the people," and the nick of time was past for a photograph. The nine sentences were spoken in five minutes, and the applause was merely formal—a tribute to the occasion, to the high office, by persons who had sat as an audience for three hours.

That evening Lincoln took the train back to Washington. He was weary, talked little, stretched out on the seats and had a wet towel laid across his forehead. He felt that about all he had given the audience was ordinary, garden-variety, dedicatory remarks. "That speech," he said, "was a flat failure, and the people are disappointed."

Much of the newspaper reaction was more condemnatory. The *Patriot and Union* of nearby Harrisburg took its fling: "The President acted without sense and without constraint in a panorama that was gotten up more for the benefit of his party than for the honor of the dead. ... We pass over the silly remarks of the President; for the credit of the nation we are willing that the veil of oblivion shall be dropped over them and that they shall no more be repeated or thought of." And the Chicago *Times* fumed: "The cheek of every American must tingle with shame as he reads the silly, flat and dish-watery utterances of the man who has to be pointed out to intelligent foreigners as the President of the United States." Wrote the correspondent of the London *Times*, "Anything more dull and commonplace it would not be easy to produce."

A reporter for the Chicago *Tribune*, however, telegraphed a prophetic sentence: "The dedicatory remarks of President Lincoln will live among the annals of man." The Philadelphia *Evening Bulletin* said thousands who would not read the elaborate oration of Mr.

> "The few words of the President were from the heart to the heart," said *Harper's Weekly.* They can't be read "without kindling emotion."

Everett would read the President's few words "and not many will do it without a moistening of the eye and a swelling of the heart." And a writer in *Harper's Weekly*: "The oration by Mr. Everett was smooth and cold. ... The few words of the President were from the heart to the heart. They cannot be read, even, without kindling emotion. 'The world will little note nor long remember what we say here, but it can never forget what they did here.' It was as simple and felicitous and earnest a word as was ever spoken."

Everett's opinion of the speech, written in a note to Lincoln the next day, was more than mere courtesy: "I should be glad if I could flatter myself that I came as near to the central idea of the occasion in two hours as you did in two minutes." Lincoln's immediate reply: "In our respective parts you could not have been excused to make a short address, nor I a long one. I am pleased to know that, in your judgment, the little I did say was not entirely a failure." ■

# THE Colonel & The King

Weak and weary, Elvis Presley promised to change. He said he'd fire his manipulative manager, but never got the chance.

By Alanna
Nash

O n the sweltering evening of August 15, 1977, Elvis Presley slipped out of his blue silk lounging pajamas. With the help of his cousin Billy Smith, he climbed into a black sweat suit, a white silk shirt and black patent leather boots, unzipped due to the puffy buildup of fluid in his ankles.

Around 10:30, after a night of motorcycle riding with his girlfriend, Ginger Alden, the singer stuffed two .45-caliber automatic pistols in the waistband of his sweatpants. Then

he donned his custom-made chrome sunglasses and slid behind the wheel of his Stutz automobile. With Alden, Smith and entourage member Charlie Hodge in tow, Elvis drove to the office of his dentist in East Memphis. A few of Presley's teeth needed fixing, and he wanted to tend to them before he left the following night for Portland, Maine, the first day of a 12-day tour.

When the group returned to Graceland near midnight, Elvis and Ginger went upstairs, and Smith retired to his trailer on the property. Sometime around 2 a.m., Elvis spoke with Larry Geller, perhaps his closest friend. Geller recalled that Elvis was "in a very good mood, looking forward to the tour, making plans for the future." About 4 a.m., Elvis felt energetic enough for a racquetball game and called Billy and his wife, Jo, to join him and Ginger. As they went out to Elvis's private court, a light rain began to fall.

"Ain't no problem. I'll take care of it," Elvis said and put out his hands as if to stop it. Miraculously, Smith remembered, the rain let up. "See, I told you," Elvis said. "If you've got a little faith, you can stop the rain."

Despite his sudden burst of energy, Elvis was exhausted from several days of a Jell-O diet, the latest in a series of desperate attempts to trim down enough to fit into his stage costumes. He tired quickly on the court, and they quit.

Upstairs in the house, Smith washed and dried his cousin's hair. As they talked, Elvis obsessed about a new book that detailed his physical deterioration. The book disclosed just how dependent on drugs—mostly amphetamines and sedatives—the King had become. Elvis fumed that he'd bring the authors—his former bodyguards Red West, Sonny West and Dave Hebler—to Graceland, where he'd kill them himself and dispose of their bodies. He couldn't understand how they could have betrayed him. Then his mood dimmed, and he rehearsed a speech he planned to give from the stage if his fans, shocked to learn their idol spent about $1 million a year on his prescription drug habit, booed him in concert. "They've never beat me before," he said, "and they won't beat me now." Billy knew what he meant: "Even if I have to get up there and admit to everything."

Numb and weary, Elvis began to cry. "It's okay," Billy soothed. "It's going to be all right." As Smith went out the door, Elvis turned to him and said, "Billy ... son ... this is going to be

my best tour ever." At 7:45 a.m., the singer downed four or five sleeping pills, his second such dose in a couple of hours. Elvis had long been plagued by sleep troubles, beginning when he was a child and escalating with his drug-taking and rock-star hours. A third dose would soon follow. He'd eaten no solid food since the day before.

Sometime around 8 a.m., Elvis climbed into bed with Ginger. The Memphis beauty queen, then in her early 20s, recalled that she awoke to find her aging boyfriend too keyed up to sleep, preoccupied with the tour. "Precious," Elvis said, "I'm going to go to the bathroom and read for a while."

Ginger stirred. "Okay," she said, "but don't fall asleep."

"Don't worry, I won't," he said. Behind the bathroom door, Elvis picked up *The Scientific Search for the Faces of Jesus*, a book about the Shroud of Turin, and waited for his pharmaceutical escort to slumber.

**As Elvis's day was ending in Memphis,** Col. Tom Parker's was already in full swing in Portland. Parker had managed Elvis's career since the mid-1950s and gradually had taken over nearly every aspect of the star's life. From time to time Elvis spouted off about the Colonel's incessant interference. But when Parker put his foot down, Elvis became docile again.

Now, on the eve of the tour, Parker was holed up in a Sheraton hotel in Portland, riding herd on his men.

At 2:20 in the afternoon, Ginger turned over in Elvis's huge bed and found it empty. Had he never come back to sleep? She noticed that his reading light was still on. Ginger knocked on the bathroom door. "Elvis, honey?"

There was no response. She turned the knob and went inside. Elvis was slumped on the floor.

Ginger bent down to touch him. He was cold, his swollen face buried in the red shag carpet, blood dotting his nostrils. His skin was mottled purple-black.

Soon, an ambulance screamed up the drive. The upstairs became filled with people: Charlie Hodge, crying and begging Elvis not to die; Elvis's father, Vernon, collapsing on the floor; Elvis's daughter, 9-year-old Lisa Marie, who was visiting from California, peering wide-eyed into the scene.

"What happened to him?" asked one of the EMTs, Ulysses Jones.

Entourage member Al Strada blurted out the truth. "We think he OD'd."

At Baptist Memorial Hospital, the emergency team did its best. But no measure, whether frantic or heroic, could save Graceland's master. Elvis Presley was dead at the age of 42.

**From the hospital, an Elvis aide, Joe Esposito, called the Colonel in Maine.** "I have something terrible to tell you," Joe began, his voice wavering. "Elvis is dead."

Thirty seconds, maybe more, passed before Parker spoke. "Okay, Joe," the manager finally said, his voice flat, devoid of emotion. "We'll be there as soon as we can." Esposito sensed that beneath the calm, the Colonel was shaken.

Within minutes the Colonel's men were summoned to his hotel room. They were shattered but hardly surprised. For months now, the most celebrated performer in the world had barely been able to find his way to the microphone. Elvis himself had a good idea of his condition. Not long before, he'd invited the songwriter Ben Weisman to his suite in Vegas. His face puffy, Elvis sat down at the piano.

> # Elvis had never been so sick. But the cigar-chomping Colonel thundered, "The only thing that's important is that he's on the stage tonight."

"Ben," he said, "there's a song I love, 'Softly As I Leave You.' But it's not about a man leaving a lady. It's about a man who's going to die."

The Colonel had seen irrefutable evidence of Elvis's condition as late as May 21, 1977, in Louisville. Larry Geller was in the anteroom of Elvis's hotel suite, waiting for Dr. Nick—Dr. George Nichopoulos, Elvis's primary doctor—to finish administering drugs that would transform Elvis from a sick, lethargic man to an energized performer. Suddenly, an angry Tom Parker appeared. "I'm going in," the Colonel said curtly, brushing past Geller.

Parker opened the door to a devastating sight—Elvis, semiconscious and moaning, with Dr. Nick working frantically to revive him. At first Geller's heart sank. Then he felt relieved. Finally, the Colonel was seeing Elvis at his worst. The star had never been so out of it, so sick. Surely now the Colonel would pull him off the road, get him help. Instead, Parker thundered out of the room. "You listen to me!" he shouted at Geller, stabbing the air with his cane.

"The only thing that's important is that he's on that stage tonight!" Now, on August 16, while Elvis's most devoted fans began a pilgrimage to Memphis from all points of the globe, the Colonel booked a flight, not to Tennessee but to New York. There, he met with RCA, for whom his client had sold more tapes and records than any other performer in history. Rightly expecting that every store in the country would sell out of Presley products within 24 hours, Parker put the squeeze on RCA to engage the major record-pressing plants at premium prices—shoving other orders

aside—to keep a rich river of Elvis records churning. Next Parker met with a merchandiser, cutting a deal for Elvis tie-ins. Only then did he travel to Memphis for Elvis's funeral service on August 18.

**Tom Parker was born Andreas Cornelis van Kuijk** in 1909 in Breda, Holland. One day in May 1929, his family received a mysterious letter, saying he'd gone away but giving no details of his whereabouts. He signed his subsequent notes "Andre" or "Thomas Parker."

Who in the world was Thomas Parker? Three decades would pass before the family learned the answer. By then Parker had joined the U.S. Army, gone AWOL, been hospitalized for psychological disturbances, received a discharge and emerged anew as an ambitious talent agent with the honorary title of "Colonel."

For a while Parker managed the popular crooner Eddy Arnold. But when Arnold summarily fired him in 1953, Parker, desperate for a major new client, was soon taking note of a young and hip Elvis Presley.

Parker turned up at a Presley show in Texarkana. Bob Neal, who had been booking Elvis in the region, certainly wanted to work something out with Parker, hoping this "razzle-dazzle character," as he called the Colonel, would put Elvis on package tours around the country.

It wasn't until Elvis's appearance in May 1955, before 14,000 fans in Jacksonville, Fla., that Parker realized what he had. "Girls, I'll see you all backstage," Elvis joked at the end of the show, and about half the crowd broke through the police barricade, a throng following him into the locker room, trying to tear off his clothes.

Parker now understood that Elvis's popularity could go beyond anything he'd ever seen. Enlisting the help of RCA Victor and the William Morris Agency, Parker took no more than a year to make Elvis the biggest-selling artist in the music business. The Colonel accepted a nearly $40,000 advance from a Beverly Hills merchandiser to turn Elvis into a brand name, licensing 78 different articles—from Elvis charm bracelets and lipstick in "Hound Dog" orange to scarves, dolls and glow-in-the-dark busts. That entrepreneurial vision raked in some $22 million, apart from what fans spent on concerts and records. No artist had ever exploded on the scene with the volcanic impact of Elvis Presley in 1956. No longer just a mere musical phenom, he would become perhaps the most influential cultural figure of the 20th century.

**A full 82 percent of all American TV sets** were tuned in to "The Ed Sullivan Show" on September 9, 1956— the first night of Elvis's three guest shots. The Colonel also had his sights on the big screen. Elvis's first film, *Love Me Tender*, opened at New York's Paramount Theater on November 15, 1956, a 40-foot cutout of the star decorating its façade. Nearly 2,000 fans of all ages lined up, the queue snaking for blocks. The theater manager sent the film studio's publicity department an ecstatic telegram: "Spread the news that we have a most sensational attraction!"

Parker had staged the gathering as a publicity stunt. They were a team: Presley providing the talent, and Parker, through ingenuity, converting the talent into one of the most amazing careers in show business.

Not all was well with Elvis, however. The 21-year-old star had begun telling reporters that the hysteria at his concerts "makes me want to cry." Everything had gotten so big so fast. And now the Army was making noises about drafting him. On Easter Sunday 1957, when he should have been enjoying his new mansion, Graceland, Elvis told his minister, the Reverend James Hamill, "I am the most miserable young man you have ever seen."

But the Colonel was all business. Consumed with manipulating Elvis's military service for the greatest public relations good, Parker made Elvis this promise: "If you go into the Army, stay a good boy and do nothing to embarrass your country, I'll see to it that you'll come back a bigger star than when you left."

**Serving at Fort Hood, near Killeen, Texas,** in 1958 Elvis had a haunting dream: When he came out of the Army, everything was gone—no songs on the charts, no fans in the audience. Elvis had long pilfered diet pills from his mother, Gladys. When Gladys's health began rapidly declining—a doctor diagnosed hepatitis—and she died in August 1958 at age 46, Elvis was inconsolable. Feeling isolated and anxious, he was soon on his way toward developing a serious prescription drug habit, aided by physicians and friends over the years.

After Elvis sailed for Germany, the Colonel wrote him long, chatty letters designed to fill him in on his efforts "to keep your name hot over here" and to try to boost the singer's spirits. Parker reported spectacular results. His hard work, he wrote, combined with his diverse promotions—some $3 million from souvenirs alone—would bring in more revenue for 1958 than the year before, even though Elvis was in the service. Parker was also finalizing lucrative movie deals.

Elvis came home from Europe a more licentious man than the boy who'd left. His familiarity with pills, especially uppers, had become an obsession, and he talked of buying his own drugstore for a steady supply. His behavior, fueled by a steady stream of pills, was becoming erratic. His temper erupted, and one night he broke down, saying he felt boxed in by his lightweight movies. In recording sessions, he could barely hide his discomfort at the bland pop songs he was being given, like "(There's) No Room to Rhumba in a Sports Car." The constant frustrations took their toll. By the 1970s—even after he'd married Priscilla and had his daughter, Lisa Marie—his drug regimen for road tours was so specific that Dr. Nick prescribed it in six stages. The drugs included testosterone, amphetamines, Dilaudid, Dexedrine and Demerol, as well as Quaalude and Amytal, hypnotic sleeping medications.

The public believed that Elvis was simply ill. By 1975, his physical problems included blood clots, hypoglycemia and an enlarged heart. His liver was more than twice the normal size, his colon distended. His weight, on a diet of junk food and downers, had zoomed from 175 pounds to 245 pounds in three years, something he tried to camouflage with darker jumpsuits and an elastic corset.

**Earlier in his career, Elvis had confessed** to his friend Larry Geller that he felt "chosen" but didn't know why. "I've always felt this unseen hand guiding my life since I was a little boy," he told Geller. "Why was I plucked out of all the millions of lives to be Elvis? There has to be a reason."

Geller had tried to help Presley in his quest to find the divinity within, sharing books and spiritual advice. Years later, when Elvis desperately needed rest—his divorce from Priscilla seemed to weaken his resolve and usher in a new

> "Girls, I'll see you all backstage," Elvis joked, and about half the crowd broke through the police barricade, trying to tear off his clothes.

round of drug use, friends said—Geller suggested foods and vitamins to strengthen Elvis's immune system. In March 1977, Elvis vowed to take time off and restore his well-being. He pledged other changes in his life as well. "He was adamant about firing the Colonel," said Geller, recalling that Elvis told him, "Larry, I promise you, this is what I'm going to do." He would see to it, he said, by the end of the summer. But the chance to break free never came.

British journalist Christopher Hutchins interviewed Tom Parker in 1993, four years before the wily old manager passed away. Wasn't Elvis the son the Colonel never had? Hutchins probed. "I have to be honest," Parker answered. "I never looked on him as a son. But he was the success I always wanted." ∎

# The Day the Bears Go to Bed

By Jean George

How do these animals know when it's time to dig dens and hibernate? Three scientists search for clues to one of nature's grand mysteries.

Her grave face turned into the wind, the female grizzly bear jogged swiftly though a lonely lodgepole-pine forest in Yellowstone National Park. Snow was gusting around her that November 5, 1963, when she reached her den at the base of a fir tree. For a moment the behemoth hesitated; then she pushed her head beneath the fir roots and shuffled in.

Sinking down on a bed of boughs she had gathered days before, she fitted her back into the rounded earth, rolled her nose into her belly and covered her head with her paws. Her body relaxed, she growled softly and began to pass into the deep and mysterious sleep that would lower her temperature and slow down her

ILLUSTRATION BY ANITA KUNZ

heartbeat and breathing. In hibernation, a state devised by nature for protection, she could live through Yellowstone's cold and foodless winter.

Unknown to the grizzled sleeper, a small radio transmitter in a yellow plastic collar around her neck beeped on. Three scientists, following the beeps, trudged up the steep slope in the spinning snow. Then the signal weakened; it could barely penetrate the earth from the den. Dr. Frank Craighead, Jr., a naturalist, president of Environmental Research Institute, grinned at his snow-covered companions, Dr. John Craighead and Maurice Hornocker. "She's in. The old gal's gone to bed!" Five years of work had come to a victorious climax. For the first time in history a grizzly bear had been successfully tracked into its hibernation den by radio.

Frank scanned the blue-white wilderness near Trout Creek to see what signs had told the bear that tomorrow's dawn would rise on a snow-locked world that would not release its grip until spring. Although the snow was whiting out the canyons and forest that day, and the great gray owl huddled somewhere against a tree, these signs of winter had come before during Yellowstone's erratic autumn. Each time they had said winter to the men, but not to the bears, who had stayed up, knowing by some mysterious sense that these preliminary snows would soon melt and the air would warm above freezing.

But today all the grizzlies on the Yellowstone plateau would go to bed—hundreds of them. The Craighead brothers knew from previous years that when darkness came this night, every grizzly bear in the Park would be snowed under the roots of some lonely tree. Yet the country looked for all the world like any other snowy day in autumn. Why had the bears chosen this day? And which of the components of the day—temperature, barometric pressure, vanishing food supply, snow—had triggered the biological clocks in the bears? Or had these environmental stimuli only appeared to put the clocks in action? The Craigheads and their team of scientists felt that they could not answer some of these questions.

That day ended the fifth year in a seven-year study of the grizzly bear, *Ursus horribilis,* conducted by the Craigheads. Sons of a naturalist in a family of naturalists, they had grown up in Washington, D.C. Their lives were literally cliffhangers, from dropping down canyon sides on ropes to study eagle and falcon eyries, to being abandoned on a Pacific atoll by the U.S. Navy as part of a research project on survival in the jungle. It was on that island that they decided they would work together, through wildlife research, to help keep intact the natural environment man needs for his physical and spiritual welfare.

When, years later, they learned that the grizzly bear was vanishing from the West, they urged the National Geographic Society, the National Science Foundation, Philco Radio Corp. and the U.S. Fish and Wildlife Service to help them make a comprehensive study of the bears in Yellowstone. The information they and their team of doctors,

physicists, engineers and biologists uncovered is now being used to give the grizzly the kind of management it needs for roaming and denning, for food and shelter.

The Craigheads were among the first to employ the new space science of bio-telemetry, gathering distant information on animals through radio transmitters and receivers. Frank said of the technique, "The bears wander far into inaccessible country, and they are most active at night. We could not follow or consistently observe them without radios."

Even with bio-telemetry, facts were not easy to get. The bears had to be trapped, anesthetized and color-tagged for identification—by snapping numbered plastic tags of different colors into each ear. Then the enormous animals had to be weighed, measured, sexed. Several were fitted with collars carrying the transmitters that pulsed at different rates for each individual.

Four of the instrumented bears were monitored from the laboratory in Canyon Village, where the radio beeps could be picked up for a distance of 12 miles, 24 hours a day. The others could be monitored at will by receivers in the field. When a transmitter began to give off odd sounds, the Craigheads would get compass bearings, hike sometimes ten miles into the dense forests to see what the sounds meant. An on-off signal was found to be a bear digging or entering a den, an irregular signal indicated walking and moving around and a continuous rhythmic beep was a nap.

A strong trap made from heavy steel sewer piping and a dart that injected a drug were used to capture the bears. The anesthesia had to be carefully administered as there were no known dosages for bears. Once, when a cub got too much, John had to give him artificial respiration. Also, there were some radio troubles. One bear sat down in a stream and shorted her transmitter. Eventually, however, some 300 grizzlies cooperated by walking into traps.

Several summers ago I drove with the Craigheads toward a bear that had just been trapped. He was put to sleep, then lifted out of the trap by four men and placed in a cargo net. When he was cranked slowly up for weighing, the scale read 500 pounds. "Just a little one," Frank said, as they tagged the bear, measured his ears and body length and took a blood sample. Meanwhile, the crew was making imprints of the bear's glistening teeth and paws in plastic, from which a technique to determine age was developed. Then Bear 114's eyes opened! In a few minutes he sat up, shook his head and arose. Although some bears would charge the team of men, this one just gave us a bored glance and then hurried off.

In the laboratory in Canyon Village, bear-paw imprints, maps and radios lay on the long tables. A map for each bear hung on the walls. As the men tuned in on the bears, their locations were marked on the maps. Eventually their home ranges were obtained in this way. Some had large ranges, 14 miles by four. Another bear, No. 40, required only five miles by three in which to eat and nap.

By 1965, the Craigheads were on their way toward understanding the secrets of prehibernation. They knew that the bears went off to bed simultaneously but on a different calendar day of each year studied: October 21–22 in 1961, November 5, 1963, and November 11, 1965. All were days of storm, cold and low barometric pressure.

The dens were warm and ingeniously chosen. Some were located on slopes that could be death traps to humans when the snow came; some were on canyon walls. All were on slopes facing north, exposures that did not thaw during the brief warm spells. All were dug by the bears themselves under the roots of big trees. No den found was ever used the following season.

All the dens were lined with pine and fir boughs, the region's best insulation, raked down by the bears and carried to their dens in their teeth. It seemed that expectant females fashioned deeper and softer bough beds than barren females and boars; and the cubs, conceived in June, were born to a drowsy mother who may have snoozed through the process in December.

The bears know that the day is coming and prepare their cavities many weeks ahead of the last storm. Then they all wait for that final trigger. In the last autumn of the study, a series of unusual weather conditions unlocked some answers to the question of what the final trigger was. Until then, winter had always come to Yellowstone gradually, in snows and thaws and slowly increasing cold before the final blow. But that September 15, when Frank was chopping wood, he noticed that the temperature was dropping swiftly. The thermometer registered 12 degrees Fahrenheit. This was unusual for September and even more so when the cold front stayed for eight bitter days. The bears, however, did not move from their summer areas.

October 15 was another unusual day. The morning dawned warm and sunny. Birds sang; rivers ran free. At noon, however, it grew cloudy, and Frank flipped on the laboratory receiver. He and assistant Bob Ruff were startled by what they heard. No. 202 had left his Sulphur Mountain summer bedding area and was clipping along Elk Antler Creek.

John tuned in on other bears. They were all on the move. 181 was splashing across the Yellowstone River; 65, a barren female, was trotting toward a canyonside. At four o'clock that afternoon, snow dropped silently on Yellowstone.

But though the bears had gone to their dens, they had not gone inside. Some were digging—a thing they never did on hibernating day. Perplexed, the brothers waited all night while the transmitters sang on. Three days later the sun came out, and the snow melted.

From that day to hibernating day was a lonely vigil in the Yellowstone wilderness. Frank tracked a sow and saw her sitting on her big haunches on an isolated ledge desperately fighting sleep. He had never seen this before. The lethargy of hibernation had set in, but she would not den. John found that her son, 202, was also having trouble. The receiver beeped as he went into his den and came out, went in and came out—waiting for something, he knew not what.

Finally, on November 11, 1965, a storm rode into Yellowstone. When Frank flipped on the receiver, erratic beeps came from the bear radios. One was giving the weak signal that meant that the bear had denned. 202, however, was some little distance from his den. Frank set out to find him. As he fought his way for six miles through dense timber, he watched the ground for tracks. 202, the receiver indicated, was close by, but Frank could not see his tracks.

> A bear was trapped, put to sleep, then lifted up by four men to be weighed. He was 500 pounds. "Just a little one," Frank said.

Then 202 was just ahead of him, marching hard. Frank watched his feet, for now he was certain of what the bears were instinctively waiting for—a drifting, blowing storm that would cover their tracks as they hurried to their dens. By morning the radios were all transmitting their "underground" signals. And there was not one bear print to tell which way the bears had gone.

In the laboratory the Craigheads put some of the facts together and speculated. The cold snap of September 15 had set off the first bell—drowsiness. A month later the second bell went off—the urge to be alone. That day grizzlies had gone off to their dens in the canyonsides and forests. They had not denned up, for the final alarm had not yet sounded—the drifting, blowing snow that erased their footsteps and sealed the plateau until spring.

As Frank looked out at the white wilderness, he thought that even though he and John and their colleagues had taken many secrets from the bears, the most awesome one remained unknown—the "feel" of that final storm that would bind the lakes in ice, slow the rivers and close the roads until spring. Perhaps that secret was theirs, forever, buried in instinct and old bear wisdom from millions of years of listening to the murmurs from the earth. ■

# RUDY
# Giuliani:

# GUTS
# Grace &
# Glory

By
Frank
Lalli

## September 11 defined Giuliani's mayoral term. His firm character and leadership impressed everybody.

udy Giuliani loves the impossible. That trait has shaped his life, prepared him to lead the nation in those horrific days after September 11 and transformed him into our most popular leader. In this interview with *Reader's Digest,* the mayor reveals how he learned to fight for what he believes in and how he overcame his worst fear. He also candidly discusses the love in his life—and God's plan for his future.

**RD: What is your first memory?**
**Giuliani:** In the late '40s, at the height of the rivalry between the New York Yankees and the Brooklyn Dodgers, we lived so close to Ebbets Field that you could hear the fans cheering. But my father was a Yankee fan. Before I had a choice, he began dressing me up in a little Yankee uniform—even my bat had Yankee pinstripes.

**RD: Was it dangerous to go around Brooklyn in a little Yankee uniform?**

**Giuliani:** That's more than a joke. And that experience has something to do with my character and personality. I had to physically defend myself from neighborhood kids who would attack me. Once they put a rope around my neck and tried to hang me from a tree. My grandmother chased them away.

**RD: Why did your father continue sending you out in the uniform?**

**Giuliani:** He thought I would learn how to stand up for what I believed in. And he turned out to be right. There are a thousand ways to teach a child that lesson, and that was his way. My father also taught me how to box, beginning when I was very young. He would sit in a chair, so as I grew up he remained my height. He would have a pair of boxing gloves on, and I would have a pair. And he would tell me to try to hit him. Then he would show me how to defend myself; he would never hit me.

**RD: What did your mother say?**

**Giuliani:** That he was going to make me too violent. So in response, he would always lecture me, saying I shouldn't be a bully, shouldn't be an aggressor and should never fight with anyone smaller than me.

**RD: Did his lessons sink in?**

**Giuliani:** Yes, they did. Let me fast-forward to September 11. All that day, I could hear him saying to me, "In crisis, when everybody else gets very, very excited, you have to become the calmest person in the room, so you can figure a way out of the situation." He would say that over and over. And on September 11, his voice was in my head.

**RD: Starting with your father making you a Yankee fan in Brooklyn, you have achieved the unachievable—crushing the mob when you were a prosecutor, becoming a Republican mayor of a Democratic stronghold, and then revitalizing the city that experts had written off as the Rotting Apple.**

**Giuliani:** I love the challenge of doing things people say can't be done. The minute somebody says, "That can't be done," I respond by thinking it would be interesting, exciting and fulfilling to prove it can be done.

**RD: Did you ever think you were facing something you couldn't beat?**

**Giuliani:** Yes, on September 11. What ignited that feeling was seeing a man jump from Tower One. An aide said people were jumping, but my mind rejected it. Then, as I walked closer to the towers, a police officer told me to look up, keep looking up, so nothing would hit us. Suddenly, I see a man hurl himself from above the 100th floor and come flying down. I followed that from beginning to end. And I grabbed Police Commissioner Bernie Kerik's arm and said, "We're in uncharted territory. We're going to have to invent a way to get through this."

**RD: How did you fight your fears?**

**Giuliani:** The feeling reemerged when the first tower came down. I feared we might be attacked again, maybe later that day. I kept asking the police commissioner, "Have we thought about the Statue of Liberty, the Stock Exchange, the Empire State Building?" And then I started addressing, How am I going to explain this to people? Then, I thought of Winston Churchill. If the people of Britain could get through months of bombing during World War II, we can get through a day or two of this. That comforted me. I said, That's how I'll explain it to the people: This is not unprecedented, people have gotten through this before, and we're just as good as they were. I knew all Americans—not just New Yorkers—would respond to that message.

**RD: During that terrible day, in a sense, you were alone at the national microphone delivering that message. How did that happen?**

**Giuliani:** I was there. I was the mayor of New York. My whole approach as mayor was to be there and to be in charge. If I had not gone on TV, it would have been worse for the city. After the first tower collapsed, my press office was inundated with calls from reporters saying we understand the mayor is dead.

> "Then, I thought of Winston Churchill. If the people of Britain could get through months of bombing during World War II, we can get through a day or two of this."

**RD: Why did the press think that?**

**Giuliani:** We were missing for 20 minutes. Someone saw us go into a building, then that building got hit with debris as the first tower fell, and they never saw us come out. They didn't know we got out on another street. So when I got to the microphones, I was saying, "I'm here and I'm okay, and the city's here and the city's okay." I had to balance being honest and being hopeful. I had to say this is a horrible, awful, terrible thing, but somehow we're going to get through this. Maybe it's similar to Churchill telling his people he had nothing to offer but blood, sweat and tears. If he had said, "The Nazis are bombing us, no problem," his people would have said, "You're crazy. Go smoke one of your cigars; you're retired."

**RD: What gave you hope?**

**Giuliani:** Two things. One was the brave way people were evacuating. They were rushing, but they weren't knocking each other over. Many were stopping to help people. That said to me their spirit hadn't been broken. And the second was when I saw the newspaper photo of the firefighters putting our flag up. It looked like Iwo Jima. That brave act gave me a great sense that the American spirit is as strong as it ever was. The debris was five to seven stories high; the fires were at 2,500 to 3,000 degrees Fahrenheit. They were standing on top of hell when they put up that flag.

**RD: How long did Ground Zero remain that dangerous?**

**Giuliani:** For weeks. I wanted President Bush to come, and he did on that Friday. But I was very worried. When the President got up with the firemen, he was standing on a mound of debris. I know [laughs] the Secret Service wanted to tackle him and bring him down.

**RD: What were you thinking during the days after the attack?**

**Giuliani:** Many, many times I thought about my last conversation with my father, when he was dying of cancer. I wanted to know if he had ever been afraid during his life. He said, "I was always afraid." And then he said, "Courage is doing what you have to do even though you are afraid."

**RD: That sounds like Churchill.**

**Giuliani:** Then he added, "If you're not afraid at times, you're crazy."

**RD: And that sounds like a guy from Brooklyn.**

**Giuliani:** And I gave him a hug and gave him a kiss. My father probably had delivered that message about courage to me in other ways for the last ten years. But saying it that way right before he died had a very, very big impact on me. Since then, I've always understood that courage is about the management of fear, not the absence of fear.

**RD: When you were diagnosed with prostate cancer two years ago, what went through your mind?**

**Giuliani:** It made me ask questions about life, death and mortality that ultimately helped me get through September 11. I concluded that everyone lives every day with the possibility of dying. People with cancer just confront it more dramatically.

**RD: Were you ever as frightened?**

**Giuliani:** No. No, no, no, no. Because it's lonely. You have to come to terms with a deadly disease. But during the time I was diagnosed with prostate cancer, incredible numbers of people died of all different things, including the awful tragedy of September 11. Getting cancer is just another way of having to deal with the human situation.

**RD: Soon after you faced your own mortality, the public's response to your leadership on September 11 gave you a measure of immortality.**

**Giuliani:** Right. But it's hard for me to accept that. Sometimes people wave, yelling, "Rudy, way to go, Rudy." I say to myself, "Why are these people waving at me?"

**RD: What do you make of the mass response to the tribute to victims at the Metropolitan Opera?**

**Giuliani:** The head of the Met told me the company wanted to stage a benefit performance on September 22 and asked if I'd speak. When I arrived, I realized they had put a giant TV screen in the plaza in front of the opera house, so the public could see the performance. But people were not going out then, so there was concern. If only five people showed up, that could send a counterproductive message: Everybody's scared. At intermission, I walked outside and there were thousands of people. That crystallized something for me. People weren't going out—but not because of fear. They were mourning.

**RD: And you got a standing ovation that went on for five minutes.**

**Giuliani:** Almost as long as Caruso and Plácido Domingo and Luciano Pavarotti—but never as long [laughing]. It was a great experience, like the wedding. Those events helped me see that the beautiful things in life have to go on. Otherwise, the terrorists win.

**RD: At several 9/11 funerals, you addressed the children of fallen firemen and policemen. You said that in one sense they had gotten a gift. They now knew—and would know forever—that their father was a great man. Now your son, Andrew, and daughter, Caroline, know you are being hailed as a great man, too. Do you worry they might feel pressure to live up to your hero's image?**

**Giuliani:** It's hard for me to think of myself as a great man. I don't accept that. I have never wanted my children to feel they had to live their lives in a particular way—or that they had to compete with me in any way. My mother and father taught me, "Find something you enjoy doing, and you will be happy." That's what I tell my children. And not just tell them—I try to conduct myself in a way that allows them to find their own path to happiness.

**RD: Have you talked to Andrew or Caroline about this since 9/11?**
**Giuliani:** [Laughing] No. My son, who is now 16, is much more interested in meeting ballplayers—his real heroes—than talking to me. And while I was mayor, my 12-year-old daughter was most impressed that I met *NSYNC. That's the way kids are, if you don't distort them.

**RD: Perhaps overcompensating for his background, your father insisted that you never cheat, nor lie—to the point where he overdid it. Do you try to avoid overdoing it with your son and daughter?**
**Giuliani:** My father constantly put tremendous pressure on me about being honest about everything. My mother had a different way. You could never meet her expectations. If you came home with a 90, she'd say, "How come it's not 95?" If you got 100, "How come you didn't get all 100s?" That was her imperfect way of motivating. So when I see my kids' report cards, I give them positive reinforcement. I don't want to put extraordinary pressure on them. Some parents make their children believe that whatever happens is so crucial, and it really isn't. Children's lives are not determined in their tenth year or fifteenth year or by whether they get into the right college or have one bad year in school. I think too much pressure is put on kids to be perfect.

**RD: How will New York City react if it is attacked again?**
**Giuliani:** New York is going to be here forever, and the people of the city will do what they have to do to get through whatever happens.

**RD: What makes you so confident?**
**Giuliani:** People who live in freedom are stronger than any terrorists. They are operating out of hatred and maniacal anger that ultimately will destroy them. Hitler did tremendous damage, but he didn't win. Our idea of freedom and democracy are right. I don't mean this in a belligerent way. I mean it in a moral and philosophical way: We're right, and they're wrong. That doesn't mean all our ideas are right, or that we're always right. But our philosophy is correct; their philosophy is warped. Ultimately, many more people will follow our way of life than theirs.

**RD: Is this generation ready for the challenges ahead?**
**Giuliani:** I remember reading Tom Brokaw's book about the World War II generation [*The Greatest Generation*] and thinking, I'm pretty sure we would have the same strength. But, you don't know—just as you don't know what you might do. But on September 11, I knew we were strong enough. This generation is no different than the one that fought the Second World War because the same set of beliefs—the same core values—motivates us. That's why we'll prevail, as we always have.

**RD: You attended Catholic schools and even thought about becoming a priest. Who was your favorite saint?**
**Giuliani:** St. Francis because of his kindness and humanity. I often think of Father [Mychal] Judge [the Fire Department chaplain who died at Ground Zero]. Sometimes I would see him in his Franciscan robes and sandals and sometimes in his fireman's uniform. To me, he embodied the ideal blend of spirituality and public service. Growing up, I learned about leadership by reading the biographies of political leaders, like Churchill, and saints, like St. Francis. I have prayed to St. Francis from kindergarten on.

**RD: Did you pray on September 11?**
**Giuliani:** I pray at night when I go to bed—not every night, though maybe I should [laughing]. But during September 11 and after, I found myself praying in the middle of the day, asking God to help me do the right thing. I became intensely religious trying to figure things out. Why did one man live and another die? The building we were in could have been crushed by the first tower. When you contemplate those questions—the mysteries of life—it humbles you. It drives you to your knees.

**RD: You have said that God spared you for a purpose.**
**Giuliani:** God has a plan, even when you don't understand it fully. But you do have a sense of it, and you have a choice. You can conduct yourself in accordance with it or not. You can either do good or bad. I am trying to devote my life to as many good purposes as possible.

**RD: How will you do good?**
**Giuliani:** I believe you do good in concentric circles, beginning with the people you support and who support you. I have a very big family [laughing], including all the people who served with me in government and now work with me in our consulting business. I also am spending more time with my children. And September 11 has made me much closer to Judith [his companion then and later his wife, Judith Nathan]. We were close already. And then we went through hell together. In addition, I feel a special responsibility to protect the families of the fallen firemen and policemen through the Twin Towers Fund.

**RD: Will you run for office again?**
**Giuliani:** When I was younger I set my sights on specific jobs, like U.S. Attorney, mayor. But my prostate cancer and September 11 have changed me. I'm going to let that decision come into focus in the next year or two. The possibilities are far more exciting that way. I do see myself in public office. I just don't know where or when. ■

**I WAS FILLING IN** as receptionist at my husband's dental office when a patient called to cancel an appointment because, he said, he felt a migraine coming on. "You should talk to my husband," I offered. "He gets migraines, too, but has a prescription he takes before the headaches immobilize him." I also advised, "It might be helpful if you have a cola drink right away."

The patient thanked me and said he might talk to my husband later. After he hung up, my husband asked me, "Who was that?"

I told him the man's name. "Oh yeah?" said my husband. "He's the head of neurology at the university hospital."

-JAN FOULGER TINGEY

**MY HUSBAND,** Jeff, and I incurred several problems while assembling our new computer system, so we called the help desk. The man on the phone started to talk to Jeff in computer jargon, which confused us even more. "Sir," my husband politely said, "please explain what I should do as if I were a 4-year-old."

"Okay," the computer technician replied. "Son, could you please put your mommy on the phone?"

-LENA WORTH

**THE REPORTER** at the desk next to mine was excited about an upcoming assignment. All week Summer had been preparing to interview a woman known as a psychic. She wasn't sure how seriously to take the woman's supposed powers.

"Should I have a reading done?" Summer wondered. "What if it's bad news, like I'm going to die or something?"

But the morning of the interview, the psychic called. She was going to have to postpone the interview, she said. Something unexpected had come up.

-ROBERT CARROLL

**MY 21-YEAR-OLD DAUGHTER,** Jamie, landed an internship with a prestigious engineering firm in the city. I was proud, but worried about her finding a place to park on her first day, so I asked her to call when she got settled. "Mom, I can't do that," she said. "I don't even know if I'll have my own desk, let alone be able to phone."

"Nonsense," I replied. "You're a capable young professional in a demanding field. You'll have to speak up and take charge. Just march up to your boss and tell him you have to call your mother."

-JAN KIESLER

**AS A JUDGE,** I was sentencing criminal defendants when I saw a vaguely familiar face. I reviewed his record and found that the man was a career criminal, except for a five-year period in which there were no convictions.

"Milton," I asked, puzzled, "how is it you were able to stay out of trouble for those five years?"

"I was in prison," he answered. "You should know that—you were the one who sent me there."

"That's not possible," I said. "I wasn't even a judge then."

"No, you weren't the judge," the defendant countered, smiling mischievously. "You were my lawyer."

-PHILIP R. RILEY

**OUR FRIENDS** Kevin and Shari own a small business and recently suffered a series of calamities. Kevin was in an accident and totaled their business vehicle. A piece of electrical equipment was ruined after being struck by lightning. A storm destroyed their business sign, and the windshield of a car in their parking lot was shattered by flying debris.

As Kevin called their insurance agent for the fourth time, he said to Shari, "He's not answering."

Shari responded, "Maybe he has Caller ID."

-LYNN BARCLAY

# The Little Boy Who Couldn't CRY

When a couple decided to adopt Michael, they soon realized that he came with serious feelings of loss and betrayal.

The first time I saw the little boy who was to be my son, he was huddled on a brown vinyl couch in a psychologist's office. Pale, with dark stubbly hair and nail-bitten fingers, he sat near a silent couple in their mid-40s, his adoptive parents, I assumed. It was Wednesday, June 15, 1987. Michael was 4 years old.

My husband, Terry, and I weren't supposed to see him, but we did as we hurried by. Abandoned as a toddler by his natural mother, Michael was about to be told that he was

## By Deborah Snyder

ILLUSTRATION BY ALLISON SEIFFER

being given away again. We heard later that when the psychologist told him he'd have to leave his mommy and daddy and get a "new" mommy and daddy, he began to tremble convulsively. Then he soiled his pants.

**Terry and I had decided to adopt a child** after 13 years of marriage—and three children of our own. We enrolled in classes offered by our local department of human services and listened as Sheryl, one of the adoption workers, told us about the children available through the public agency. We heard horrifying stories of toddlers locked in closets and choked unconscious by drunken parents, and we looked at photographs that left us shaken and nauseated.

I went home from the first few meetings in tears. *I'd rather not know about this stuff*, I thought with a shudder. *Can I really deal with a child who's been through things like that?* But at the end of the course we had submitted an adoption application, stating our preference for a boy 4 to 9 years old.

> # He worried about dirty clothes. "My other mommy took away all my socks because I kept messing them up."

The wait lasted exactly nine months. Our family was vacationing in Florida when Sheryl called. "I think I've found a child for you," she said. "His name is Michael."

Then she filled in the tragic details. Michael's mother, a drug user, had repeatedly tried to give him away. He was 22 months old, still in diapers, when she abandoned him, with a broken arm and two black eyes, at a fast-food restaurant.

Michael spent over a year in foster care before being placed with a family, an arrangement that usually leads to legal adoption. But for Michael, it led to another rejection.

"He's a typical 4-year-old," Sheryl told us. "But his adoptive parents have never had children, and they don't seem to know what to expect from a little boy. They want him out of their home by Friday."

*Identifying details have been changed to protect privacy*

She paused. "I know this is short notice, but there's something very special about this child. Would you consider talking to him?"

Terry was on an extension nearby. I looked over at him; he returned my gaze, then nodded. "We'll catch the next plane," he told Sheryl. I threw down the phone and shouted for our kids to come hear the wonderful news.

We hurried home. The day after we saw that frightened little boy in the psychologist's office, Sheryl arranged a get-acquainted meeting. We were prepared for Michael to be tearful and depressed, but he seemed surprisingly cheerful.

**"Are you my new mom and dad?" he asked brightly.** "I'm supposed to move to your house tomorrow." He giggled nervously as we told him about his new brothers and sisters, but I noticed that he avoided our eyes. *He's probably afraid we won't want him*, I thought.

Friday morning, Terry and I went to pick up Michael at his adoptive home, an impressive house with flawless furnishings and an immaculate white carpet. We carried Michael's meager possessions out to our car, and then it was time for him to say a final goodbye to his parents. His smile remained fixed as his mother gave him an indifferent pat. When his father swept him up in a bear hug, however, his small chin began to quiver. He raced to our car, shouting, "Let's go!"

On the way home, Michael laughed and chattered animatedly. Only once, when he thought we couldn't hear him, did he express what he was feeling. "I wanted to tell my grandma goodbye," he whispered. Terry and I exchanged worried glances: This small stranger, our son, had a lot to deal with.

When we pulled into our driveway Michael looked taken aback: Our modest brick home was a sharp contrast to the one he had just left. The differences became even more marked when we stepped through the front door to be mobbed by three excited children and a dog; of necessity, our carpets and furniture were the sturdier, stain-resistant variety.

Michael smiled shyly as we introduced him to Lisa, 11, Rachel, 7, and Steven, 5. "A lot of kids live here," he observed. He asked where they had all lived "before this family" and seemed confused to hear that they'd always been with us.

Over the next few days, Terry and I concentrated on getting to know our new son. We discovered that his unhealthy pallor came from having rarely been allowed outdoors. He worried constantly about getting his clothes dirty. "My other mommy used to get real mad," he finally confided. "She took away all my socks because I kept messing them up, and then I could only wear socks on Sundays."

Terry was disgusted. He took Michael for a long walk around the neighborhood—and back through a muddy field. When they got home Michael was filthy but giggling.

We had expected the first few weeks to be difficult for Michael. Instead, he seemed almost casual in his acceptance of our family. He played happily with the other children and called us Mommy and Daddy with apparent ease. We were pleased—until our neighbors let us know he was calling them Mommy and Daddy as well. The words evidently held no special meaning for him.

Our first hint of real trouble came one day in late June. During breakfast Michael spilled cereal on his clothes, and I told him to go and change. When he didn't return, I walked back to his room. He was standing motionless by his dripping bedpost, watching a puddle of urine spread along the floor.

"Why did you do that?" I asked gently. He looked up with an empty expression, then dropped his eyes and stood silent.

Had he thought I was punishing him? I could only guess. But the incident was a startling reminder that our child was struggling with issues—abuse, abandonment, rejection—no 4-year-old was equipped to face.

June turned to July; by night, Michael often awoke screaming, but by day he seemed happy—remarkably even-tempered, never angry or upset. His face had taken on a healthy glow, and he seemed to enjoy a boyish camaraderie with Steven as they rode bikes, explored and played impish pranks on their sisters. Then something happened that left us deeply shaken.

I walked into the kitchen one afternoon to find Michael standing alone, a look of despair on his face—and a sharp butcher knife pressed to his stomach.

"Michael!" I shouted. "Put it down!" I lunged forward and snatched the knife, then collapsed into a nearby chair.

Hands trembling, I drew him onto my lap. "Honey, what were you doing?"

His answer was chilling: "I was wondering what it would be like to go to heaven."

That night Terry and I stayed up late talking—and praying. "What made me think we could change the life of an abused child?" I asked my husband. "Was it a mistake to think about adopting?"

"No," Terry said. "No! We can make a difference. We are making a difference."

Terry and I had come to rely strongly on our instincts as parents; we felt that, with patience, we could help Michael express the dark emotions that were troubling him. After checking with the psychologist, I decided to try a simple approach.

The next morning, I called Michael into my room. "Let's play a game," I suggested. "Let's try pretending we're very, very sad."

"That's a funny game," he observed, becoming immediately restrictive. He had, after all, been probed by psychologists and caseworkers much of his young life.

We sat cross-legged on the bed, taking turns frowning into a hand mirror. After a few minutes I said, "Now let's tell some things that make us sad. I'll start: It makes me sad when people say mean things to each other. How about you?"

He nodded. "It makes me sad when—" Abruptly, he stopped and jumped off the bed. "I don't want to play this game," he muttered.

I knelt beside him on the carpet. "Honey, I know this is hard, but I want you to try. Can you just whisper something in my ear?"

After a moment he leaned close; I felt his warm breath. "It makes me sad when people say they don't like me anymore. And ... and go away." As he spoke, his small body began to shake.

"It's all right," I said, wrapping him in my arms, "I'll always love you." He hugged back, fiercely, but his anguished blue eyes were tearless.

> I felt his breath. "It makes me sad when people say they don't like me anymore. And ... and go away," he said. His small body began to shake.

**As the summer progressed, Terry and I worked closely with Michael.** We noticed he often smiled when he was actually angry. So we began to stop him whenever he was disguising his feelings. "It's all right to feel anger if someone hurts you," I'd tell him. "Go ahead, make a mad face." Then I'd scowl playfully, and we'd both laugh.

One day Michael stormed in from the boys' bedroom: "It's not fair! Steven took all my race cars!"

We placated him and sent him back to tell Steven to share. "I never thought I'd be so glad to hear a kid yell," said Terry, smiling.

By the end of August, Michael was able to express his anger and seemed more confident of his place in our family. But he continued to conceal his distress about the traumatic events that had led him to our home. In the ten weeks he'd been with us, he had never cried.

"I think he's really afraid of opening that last locked door," I told Terry one day as we sat drinking coffee.

"Maybe we need to force the issue," Terry suggested. "We can't let him go on like this; it's not healthy."

The opportunity arose unexpectedly one hot September afternoon. Michael was playing contentedly with some

> # "You don't have to be afraid of those sad feelings anymore. I'm going to be your Mommy forever."

blocks. "It was fun one time when my other daddy helped me build a big tower," he said. "We threw things at it until we knocked it down."

I smiled from across the room. "I'll bet you had a lot of nice times with your 'old' daddy, didn't you?"

His silence made me look up. Although he quickly averted his face, I could see his chin quivering. A moment later he leaped to his feet.

"Watch this, Mommy!" he said, forcing a laugh. He started skipping around the room, waving his arms and grinning—though his eyes were desolate.

I stopped him. "Let's talk about your 'old' father."

He tried to squirm away, but I pulled him close, then cupped his face in my hands, making him look me square in the eyes. "Those bad feelings won't go away until you talk about them," I said softly. "Can you do that?"

I sensed the deep struggle within him as he glanced wildly around the room, looking for escape. In his desperate expression I suddenly saw the infant whose cries had gone unanswered, the tot whose outstretched arms were twisted and broken. I saw the trusting 3-year-old boy who'd been told he could stay "forever" in an adoptive home and was then rejected. I saw hurt, betrayal, anger—and, beneath it all, a deep desire to be loved. Tears streamed down my face.

"Michael?" He looked numbly into my eyes. Part of me wanted to avoid, with him, the pain he was hiding from.

But I knew the time had come to topple the last barrier he'd erected around himself.

"When you were a baby," I began unsteadily, "your mother used to hit you. Once she hit you so hard she broke your arm. Then she left you somewhere all alone. How did that make you feel?"

"Sad," Michael answered in a strained voice.

I nodded tearfully. "Then you went to a foster home, and just when you were feeling happy with your new mommy and daddy, you had to leave them, too. How did that make you feel?"

His voice was barely audible. "Sad."

"And then the mommy and daddy who were supposed to adopt you decided they didn't want you after all." The words hurt to say, and I swallowed plunging on: *Michael, how did that make you feel?*

Raw anguish filled his eyes. He stared mutely.

"It's *okay*," I said, almost pleading. "You don't have to be afraid of those sad feelings anymore. I'm going to be your Mommy forever."

His eyes remained locked on mine for a moment; then, with a shuddering wail, he collapsed into my arms and began to sob with deep, wrenching gasps. I held him tight and wept with him, feeling his hot tears soaking my shirt.

**He cried for three days.** It was as if a dam had burst. He would remember the church outfit his mother hadn't let him pack, the fishing trip his "old" daddy had never taken him on and the fishing pole—the symbol of that promise—he had to leave behind. Then he would wail again. On and on, between hugs and talk, he cried.

I cried with him through each physical enactment of past pain. Slowly we began to leave it all behind.

**On November 23, 1987, Michael legally became part of our family.** He is now a bright and mischievous 8-year-old who hopes to be "either a doctor or a mailman" when he grows up. He's doing well in the second grade.

Michael's emotional breakthrough didn't solve all his problems. He's still greatly distressed by loss, grieving deeply when friends or teachers move away. But I have begun to measure his progress by his reactions to leavetakings.

Terry travels frequently on business, and at first, each time he left, Michael would be distraught. So I established a simple ritual that helps assure him: In his life with us, every parting anticipates a return.

Michael carries his dad's bag to the old pickup Terry uses as his "airport bus." Then we hug, all of us. We say goodbye. I love you. Hurry back soon. Michael and I stand outside the house and wave until the pickup is out of sight.

"Daddy's just going away on business, isn't he?" Michael asks me. "But he'll be back with us soon, right Mommy?"

"Yes," I say, the words "with us" warming my heart. *Yes, my son.* I encircle him with my arm and draw him close. ∎

**HITCHHIKING ON A DARK NIGHT,** a man sees a car coming toward him. When it stops, he hops in the passenger seat.

No one is behind the wheel. But suddenly the car starts moving. The man looks down the road and sees a curve coming up. He panics and reaches for the steering wheel. But then a hand reaches through the window and turns the wheel, smoothly navigating the turn. Paralyzed with terror, the man watches as the hand appears before every curve.

When the car finally coasts to a stop, the man gets out, runs to a bar and tells everybody about his amazing experience.

Pretty soon, two guys walk into the bar. "Look, Pete," one says, "it's the guy who got in the car while we were pushing it."

**EDDIE AND TOM** work in a warehouse. Wanting some time off, Eddie climbs up onto the rafters and hangs upside-down from his knees.

The boss comes in and asks, "What do you think you're doing?"

Eddie swings back and forth yelling, "I'm a light bulb! I'm a light bulb!"

"I think you need some time off," his boss says. "Go home."

As Eddie turns to leave, Tom follows him. "Where do you think you're going?" the boss asks.

"Well," he replies, "you can't expect me to work in the dark."

**A SCRAWNY LITTLE FELLOW** showed up at the lumber camp looking for work. "Just give me a chance to show you what I can do," he said to the head lumberjack.

"All right," said the boss. "Take your ax and cut down that redwood tree."

Five minutes later the skinny guy was back. "I cut it down," he said, "and split it up into lumber."

The boss couldn't believe his eyes. "Where did you learn to cut trees like that?"

"The Sahara," the man answered.

"The Sahara desert?"

"Desert? Oh, sure, that's what they call it now!"

**ON A STREET CORNER** in downtown Manhattan, an old woman had a cardboard booth where she sold pretzels for 25 cents each. Every day a well-dressed young man would hurry by and toss a quarter into her cup without taking a pretzel. One day as he rushed off yet again, the woman called out to him, "Just a minute, young man!"

"I know, I know," he said. "You're wondering why it is I leave a quarter every day but never take a pretzel."

"No," the woman answered, "I wanted to tell you the price has gone up to 50 cents."

**A DYING MAN** tells his doctor, lawyer and pastor, "I have $90,000 under my mattress. At my funeral I want each of you to toss an envelope with $30,000 into the grave." After telling them this, he dies.

At the funeral, each throws his envelope into the grave. Later, the pastor says, "I must confess. I needed $10,000 for my new church. So I only threw in $20,000."

The doctor admits, "I needed $20,000 for new equipment at the hospital. So I only had $10,000 in the envelope."

"Gentlemen, I'm shocked that you would ignore this man's final wish," says the lawyer. "I threw in my personal check for the full amount."

**WALKING ALONG** the beach, a man finds a bottle. He rubs it and a genie appears.

"I'll grant you three wishes," the genie says. "There's just one condition. I'm a lawyer's genie, so for every wish you make, every lawyer in the world gets the same thing, only double."

After thinking a moment, the man says, "For my first wish, I'd like $10 million."

"Lawyers will get $20 million," the genie reminds him. "What else do you want?"

"I'd love to have a red Porsche," he says. Instantly, the car appears on the beach.

"What's your last wish?"

"Well, I've always wanted to donate a kidney."

The tragic day shocked the world. Now a famous author shows why we should not have been surprised by her death.

# What Really Killed MARILYN Monroe

**By Clare Boothe Luce**

The suicide of Marilyn Monroe in August 1962 was splashed across the front pages of the world. Editorialists, critics, fellow artists, friends and foes seemed obsessed by the question of why this woman, possessing beauty, fame and money in such abundance, had so feared or hated life that she could no longer face it.

While views differed as to who or what had executed her, one villain was the most favored: Hollywood. But the easy acceptance of this view had obscured whatever meaning and moral her life and death may have. Hollywood brought her fame, money, adulation, two respected and well-known husbands (Joe DiMaggio and Arthur Miller) and the help, however belatedly sought, of competent psychiatrists. But for all these, Marilyn might have gone to her death in her 20s instead of her 30s. Indeed, fame gave her the only form of sustained emotional security she knew, or perhaps was capable of understanding.

She believed that her extraordinary power to project sex was her great gift. Her despair at the end, when she reached out for her last and lethal dose of barbiturates, was perhaps akin to that of a painter who discovers he is going blind. The mob worship of her for her pure sexuality could last only a few years longer. She was 36, and her mirror had begun to warn her.

**A girl entering her teens has intense,** secret, often lengthy encounters with a looking glass. They are a legitimate manifestation of concern for her future as wife and mother. She learns early that the male has a natural preference for young and pretty women. The more mature and emotionally secure a woman becomes, the less she turns to the looking glass for self-confidence and a sense of her own personhood.

But for a movie star who is adored for her physical attractions, the narcissistic approach to the mirror is a continuing, ever more urgent professional necessity. Her daily, often hourly encounters with "mirror, mirror on the wall," however satisfying and reassuring in the beginning, become summit meetings with her archenemy—time.

After Marilyn passed 30, her sessions with her studio mirror must have been increasingly agonizing experiences. The growing hostility and aggressiveness she began to show, the endless changes of clothes and protracted primpings in her dressing room, the vomiting just before the cameras began to grind—all these may have foreshadowed her terror of that hour when the wolf-whistling men and oohing-and-aahing women would desert her. What then would make her valuable? Who was Marilyn Monroe if not that lovely girl on the screen, that delectable creature in the mirror?

**"I feel as though it's all happening to someone right next to *me*,"** she said in one of her triumphant hours. "I'm close—I can feel it, I can hear it, but it isn't really me."

Marilyn knew who the "real me" was. But it was an admission she sought to escape. For this "real me" was one of the saddest most frightened little girls ever born— Norma Jeane Mortenson.

An ugly congeries of evil fairies—insanity, infidelity, illegitimacy, ignorance and poverty—presided over her cradle. Her mother, Mrs. Gladys Baker, was a pretty, red-haired 24-year-old Hollywood film cutter whose husband had deserted her, taking their two children with him. She then met Marilyn's father, an itinerant baker. When the child of this casual union was born on June 1, 1926, in Los Angeles, and baptized Norma Jeane Mortenson, the father was not present. He had disappeared the day Gladys Baker told him that she was pregnant.

After the first few years, her mother began to give evidence of violent mental disturbance and was committed to an institution. For the next four or five years Norma Jeane was farmed out by the County Welfare Agency to a series of foster parents, who were paid $20 a month. She was sent for a while to an orphanage. There she earned nickels by washing dishes and cleaning toilets. Compared with this rootless little orphan of the City of Angels, the fairytale Cinderella, sweeping ashes from the hearth, lived a normal, protected, happy life.

"I always felt insecure and in the way," she once said. "But most of all I felt scared."

At the age of seven or eight, in one of the foster "homes," Norma Jeane was seduced by an elderly star boarder, who gave her a nickel "not to tell." When she did tell, her foster mother severely punished her for making up lies about the "fine man." The unhealthy and confused emotional correlations she made all through her life among sex, money and guilt may have stemmed in part from this ugly encounter. Afterward, she acquired a stammer, which remained with her for life.

In her early teens, Norma Jeane discovered, to her great delight, her one dazzling gift—an exuberant, almost atomic, vital capacity to project her sexuality. "My arrival in school started everybody buzzing," she recalled. "The boys began screaming and groaning."

She married in 1942, when she was barely 16. But she and her husband separated in 1944, apparently without tears. Never having known the face of love, she was certainly incapable of giving what she herself had not experienced. Years later, during the first year of her marriage to Arthur Miller, Marilyn said, "Now for the first time, the really first time, I feel I'm not alone anymore. For the first time I have a feeling of being sheltered. It's as if I have come in out of the cold."

Young Norma Jeane was always trying to avoid the cold. Despising marriage, deeply distrustful of both men and women but nevertheless hungry for admiration, affection and acceptance, she sought "love" with what must have been a fever-pitch promiscuity. Indeed, by the time she was entering womanhood a miracle was needed to save her from a life of overt or covert prostitution. That miracle happened. Its name was Hollywood.

In 1945, she found employment as a photographer's model, bleached her hair a golden blond and played a bit part in a 20th Century Fox movie. Then, at 22, her name changed to Marilyn Monroe, she got the lead in an obscure B picture, *Ladies of the Chorus*, shot in 11 days. The movie magazines recorded a "romance" with a musical director. The failure of this romance revealed that she was already flirting with another escort—death; she made one of her several attempts at suicide. The rejection of her physical person could not have failed to trigger and intensify the feelings of unworthiness and unwantedness ingrained in her by her miserable childhood.

A big movie break came when Arthur Hornblow, Jr., and John Huston were casting a minor role in *The Asphalt Jungle* that called for an angel-faced blonde with a wickedly curvaceous figure. Marilyn was tested for the part.

"As soon as we saw her, we knew she was the one," Hornblow recalls. Hollywood was looking for the quality that would at once touch the heart, evoking tenderness, and race the blood, stirring all the senses. This was the quality of innocent depravity, and it can be found only in a female "juvenile delinquent." Marilyn had that quality. Hollywood simply recognized it.

But the picture that really made her famous was a calendar photograph of her in the nude, for which she had cheerfully posed a year earlier. The public became aware of the fact that the calendar girl was Marilyn, just as her film *Clash by Night* was about to be released. The Fox brass blew their tops and threatened to drop her. Facing the old pattern of rejection and punishment for a misdemeanor involving sex, Marilyn once more talked of suicide. But this time the "howling mob" came to her rescue. The public clamored to see more of her. Thus it was she and the public, not Hollywood, who launched her career as a Love Goddess and started her off on her years of stardom.

**A year and a half after her suicide** the question of "What killed Marilyn?" was reviewed by her third husband, playwright Arthur Miller. In his autobiographical and self-defensive play *After the Fall*, produced last January, he holds that Marilyn wrought her own destruction by insisting on seeing herself as the utterly helpless victim of her parents, her lovers and husbands, her profession and her friends—a victim who, in her own eyes, could be "saved" only by a "limitless love." One of the themes of the play is that while every man is his brother's keeper, no man can give "limitless love," not even to the loveliest and neediest of women.

There is no reason to dispute Miller's self-exculpation for the tragedy of this woman to whom for four troubled years he sincerely tried to give enough of his mind and heart to make any normal woman feel "sheltered." She was not, of course, a normal, mature woman. She was still the orphan child—the child seeking a permanent home where warmth and tenderness would always be given unconditionally by the "grown-ups," in this case by Arthur Miller. He encouraged her to seek psychiatric help and to bolster her self-esteem by developing whatever gifts she believed she might have as an actress.

Miller accurately identified some of the problems that led to her three divorces, to her many troubles with her studio and eventually to her suicide: the insatiable demands for "limitless love"; the moodiness and depression; the orgies of self-recrimination alternated with orgies of recrimination of others; the clearly self-destructive urges always boiling and seething under the mask of careless, vibrant happiness that she tried to project to the public.

Marilyn died on a Saturday night. This "love object" of millions of unknown lonely males had no date that evening. She was suffering, physically and mentally, but she evidently neither loved nor trusted anyone enough to seek help. For above all, Marilyn was profoundly suspicious of the motives of everyone in her own regard. She had an almost psychopathic fear of being "used"—financially, as she had first been used by the foster parents who tolerated her only for the $20 board money; sexually, as she was used by the star boarder; professionally, by producers and agents.

> "My arrival in school started everybody buzzing," Marilyn recalled. "The boys began screaming and groaning."

**It is interesting to reflect on what Marilyn Monroe might think** of *After the Fall*. Morbidly sensitive to exploitation, she would probably be hurt that her own husband had gone into the business of selling her, body and soul, to the public. But certainly she would be pleased to find that her "image" still packed a punch with the public. Pathetically eager at the end to be taken "seriously" on Broadway, she would be proud to find her "image" seriously presented in a dramatic work of some intellectual distinction. And later, when Hollywood makes it into a movie, Marilyn's ghostly ears will once again hear the music she loved best—the loud, lusty masculine wolf whistles of her adoring public.

For all its "corn," the simplest lesson of Marilyn's life is that children need parents, or parent substitutes, who not only love them but who love and respect each other. Without this greatest of cradle gifts—a happy home—it is all but impossible in adulthood to deal with either failure or success. ∎

# Miracle Match

Two men, strangers, needed help in order to live. Searching for a way to save them, their wives became part of heartwarming medical history.

It was the summer of 2002 when Tracy Scott figured it was about time he stopped going barefoot. He'd coped with stubbed toes, bleeding toes even, and never felt the pain or noticed the blood. No question that his diabetes was taking its toll, affecting the nerves in his feet.

He'd just been out for a swim in the Atlantic Ocean while vacationing in Maine, and he was crossing the hot blacktop, shoes in hand, to get to the family beach house. He noticed he was sliding on the kitchen floor and figured it must be wet. It was his daughter, Ashley, who saw the real problem. Tracy hadn't felt just how hot the blacktop was

## By Michael Ryan

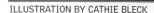
ILLUSTRATION BY CATHIE BLECK

and had second-degree burns on the bottoms of his feet. It was the blistered skin that was causing him to slip.

Tracy was 40 when he was diagnosed with insulin-dependent diabetes. His symptoms were classic. He was losing weight, but eating more than usual. He was thirsty, excessively so. And all he wanted to do was sleep. He thought he had the flu.

His wife, Robin, urged him to see his doctor. She knew diabetes ran in the family—his dad, a brother and grandfather had it. But it wasn't until he was lying on the living room floor one night, trying to watch TV with his daughters, Ashley, then 8, and Elizabeth, then 11, that he had to admit something was very wrong. Try though he might, he just couldn't manage to stay awake.

Confirmation of the diagnosis came back quickly. Tracy took it in stride. But Robin cried for days, often going off alone so Tracy and the girls wouldn't see her. She didn't want them to worry. She knew their lives were about to change and that she might lose her husband to this dread disease.

Tracy had an especially damaging form of diabetes. Still, he managed to control it for 18 months by modifying his diet and taking medication, but by then he was starting to have trouble with side effects, mostly cramping. When he finally saw a specialist, nephrologist Olga Voroshilova, he had only 30 percent function left in his kidneys. There was no question that he needed a kidney transplant.

A kidney transplant? Tracy and Robin knew all about the complications of diabetes—amputated limbs, loss of vision, premature death—but no one had ever said anything about the need for a transplant.

**For Rosario Poletta, the moment of truth came** when he realized the problems he was having—overwhelming fatigue, intense joint pain, particularly in his hands—weren't about aging or lingering sports injuries. A former high-school football player, the darkly handsome athlete was a meat cutter for a grocery store when the symptoms first appeared. The pain eventually drove him to see a specialist. The diagnosis? Lupus, an autoimmune disease that can destroy internal organs and may shorten lives. Rosario was 21 years old.

By then, "Rosie" was living in Watertown, Conn., and engaged to marry Susanna Guerrera. They'd met at a family wedding, and he'd known instantly that this bright-eyed, beautiful girl would be his wife.

Now, Rosie's doctor was warning him against marrying and said he might not be able to father children. "The doctor told me, 'You've got a beautiful girlfriend. Why do

# The doctor told Rosie, "You've got a beautiful girlfriend. Why do you want to ruin her life? She could have a beautiful life with somebody else."

you want to ruin her life? She's young. She could have a beautiful life, kids, with somebody else,'" Rosie remembers. "I called the wedding off."

But Susanna would have nothing of it. "Are you crazy?" she asked. "I knew it was going to be hard, but I was in love."

Convinced they could handle any problem together, they married before their closest friends and relatives—all 500 of them.

Six months later, Rosie's lupus flared up. A biopsy revealed his kidneys were already damaged. He would need a transplant in five to ten years.

Eleven months later, Susanna learned she was pregnant. When Tina was born, Rosie couldn't have been happier.

Six weeks later, Susanna was pregnant again. Hesitantly they mentioned it to Rosie's doctor. "Beautiful!" he exclaimed. He was about to put Rosie on a medication that would render him permanently sterile. Their timing was just right. Enter Rose, their second child in just 11 months.

For 15 years, Rosie continued to work as he battled the periodic flare-ups of lupus. With both girls in college, Susanna back at work at an insurance company and a tri-level house they had built in tranquil Watertown, Conn., the Pollettas were in a perfect place. But Rosie's body was turning on itself.

He endured drugs that made him nauseated, drugs that caused him to see double. There was a bout with bladder cancer. And then lupus began to attack his heart. It would take two angioplasties and four stents to reopen his clogged arteries.

Dr. Joseph Renda, Rosie's nephrologist, spoke frankly with the couple. His kidneys were failing. It was now time to make plans for a transplant. He looked directly at Susanna and asked, "How much do you love you husband?"

"Very much," said Susanna, not sure where this was going.

"Enough to give him a kidney?"

Susanna had never even considered the possibility, but she said yes immediately. "I'll do whatever it takes to save my husband's life."

Rosie began to cry. "No way," he said. No way would he put his kids at risk of losing both of their parents.

But Susanna had made up her mind. Their entire marriage had been a roller coaster. Her husband had kept up a cheerful front as his health worsened, but she knew how scared he was. She was going to give her kidney to him. "I loved Rosie too much to give him up," she explains.

**Robin Scott, a first-grade teacher** with a warm pulls-you-in smile, had been married to Tracy for 22 years. Of strong, stoic New England stock, she was used to the two of them handling just about anything life tossed at them. But a transplant?

She'd always thought of her husband as a vibrant, active man. Not that long ago he spent his summers splitting and stacking a six-foot-high woodpile outside their centuries-old rural Chichester, N.H., home. Now the task was beyond him. "I could see him getting weaker," she said.

Eventually he went on peritoneal dialysis. Four times a day, with Robin's help, he hooked himself up to a device that dripped fluids into his abdomen, flushing out the toxins that his kidneys could no longer process.

Tracy had been through so much: surgery to remove kidney stones; and laser surgeries on his eyes, too many to count.

His blackouts, brought on by low blood pressure and low blood sugar, were increasing in frequency and were freaking out Robin and the girls. There were days when Robin would wake up and find him passed out on the bathroom floor.

One bitter-cold morning, Tracy, a manager at a transportation company, left his office in his shirt-sleeves. He had to show one of his drivers how to make an adjustment to a van. But he started slipping into a diabetic coma. As he stumbled with his key to get back into the maintenance building, the van driver left him to get help.

No one knows how long Tracy lay outside in the frigid weather, perhaps an hour. His extremities were so cold that emergency medical technicians couldn't test his blood sugar levels. The hospital staff were able to get a reading. But his numbers were so low they thought the machine was broken.

By the time Tracy's doctor referred him to Nina Tolkoff Rubin, a medical director of dialysis and renal transplantation at Massachusetts General Hospital, Tracy was down to five percent kidney function. At best, they could

probably hold him on dialysis for another four to five years—that's how long the waiting list is for a cadaver kidney—but a transplant was inevitable.

"That's not acceptable," Robin said. She knew in her heart her husband wouldn't make five years.

Then she heard herself asking, "What if I donate?" And within 20 minutes, she was undergoing the qualifying tests.

Blood group and tissue compatibility must match to make a transplant possible. A family donor wasn't an option for Tracy, so when they learned that Robin failed to make a match, they were devastated. "We were watching our dad die," says Ashley, crying. "And there was nothing we could do."

> # Tracy's blackouts were growing more dangerous. There were days when Robin would find him passed out on the bathroom floor.

The odds for a donor kidney were poor. "There are over 55,000 people in the United States waiting for kidney transplants at any one time," says Dr. Rubin. There aren't enough cadaver donor kidneys to meet the demand, and they are more likely to fail than live donor kidneys.

Tracy tried to maintain his strength, keeping up his routines, going to work each day, even though he felt "like crap." A planner by nature, he was reduced to taking one day at a time. Robin, for her part, became increasingly anxious. It was all a matter of black and white for her. "Something more needed to be done," she says. "Our daughters and I needed to know that Tracy would be around for us."

**When he learned that his kidney function was failing rapidly,** Rosario decided it was time to call in a big favor. Bill Grize, a former colleague and a friend of his, had risen to the top of their supermarket's parent company. He had told Rosie to let him know if he was ever in trouble. The time had come.

"I called Bill and said, 'I need you,' " Rosie recalls. Grize's office contacted Mass General and came away with the name of the top transplant expert in New England. Later that same day, Rosie was talking with Dr. Rubin.

"The doctor said, 'Maybe your wife would be kind enough to donate a kidney,' " Susanna recalls. By now, Rosie had warmed to the idea. But testing showed that Susanna, like Robin, was not a good match for her husband. "I said, 'There's got to be a way you can use my kidney. My girls want a father.' "

Rubin went into overdrive looking for a solution. Working with the New England Organ Bank, she requested tissue typing of the two couples. She and a technician went over the results and discovered a surprising thing: Each wife was a good match for the other's husband. Rubin never questioned whether the couples would be willing to take the risk. She had talked to each of these women enough to know: They would do anything to give their husbands a chance at a normal life.

# The odds for a donor kidney were poor. "There are over 25,000 people in the United States waiting for kidneys at any one time," said Dr. Rubin.

**February 25, 2003, dawned cold and clear in Boston.** Despite a bitter wind, Robin and Tracy Scott, along with their two daughters, Elizabeth and Ashley, strolled the short distance from their hotel to the main entrance of Mass General. Just the four of them. Meanwhile, the Polettas had arrived with a minivan full of relatives.

The two couples then changed into light blue, polka-dotted surgical gowns before they were to gather in an L-shaped waiting room. The Polettas were telling jokes to bolster each other's spirits when Robin walked in and said right off, "I am so ready for this!"

Susanna Poletta threw her arms around Robin in an old-fashioned Italian *abbraccio*. They had met before on a previous hospital visit. "I kissed her," Susanna recalls. "It's the Italian way of saying, 'Thank you for what you're doing.' "

Tracy, though, was meeting the Polettas for the first time. He had refused to do so before, concerned that the swap might not work out. But this morning, he decided it was time. The greeting was brief, even awkward, but it was clear to all just how thankful they were for what was about to take place.

"What I was doing was giving my husband a kidney," Robin says, looking back. "It didn't feel like I was giving it to a stranger." Susanna felt the same.

It may have seemed that simple. But in fact, the two couples were about to undergo a unique, and very complicated, medical procedure. Four groups of surgeons, nurses and anesthesiologists assembled in adjoining operation rooms to begin an extraordinary choreography.

As Rosie waited to be wheeled into the OR, he fretted. "What if it doesn't work?" he asked his wife. Susanna joked back, "I'm not worried about you right now. What if it doesn't work for Tracy?"

**Susanna was the first to be summoned to surgery.** She high-fived everyone before riding down to the OR, where medical teams removed a healthy kidney from her abdomen. A second surgical team transplanted Susanna's kidney into Tracy's body, in his pelvic region, connecting it to blood vessels that extend to the leg. The remaining teams then repeated the steps, this time taking one of Robin's kidneys and transplanting it into Rosie.

This kind of four-way transfer of kidneys from two live donors to two unrelated recipients—involving four major surgeries on the same day—has only occurred a handful of times in this country. It took the courage of four individuals and the ingenuity of highly skilled medical teams to make it happen.

**All four surgeries went off without a hitch.** There's a good chance that the transplant may permanently rid Rosie of lupus. Tracy Scott says he feels great. He's on the donor list for a pancreas, however. It's his only hope of living completely free of diabetes.

The men return to Mass General for regular checkups and testing, and they have worked out matching schedules for the visits so they can see each other. The couples talk of a reunion someday, maybe a barbecue or a small intimate dinner, but they agree there's no rush.

For now, they are all just kicking back, enjoying life. Almost normal again—something they knew would happen. They just didn't know how. ■

# The Girl Who Was Anne FRANK

*By Louis de Jong*

She became the voice of the lost children of World War 11. Her diary recounting her experience hiding from the Nazis serves as a poignant reminder of the strength of the human spirit.

"And how do you know that the human race is *worth* saving?" an argumentative youngster once asked Justice Felix Frankfurter.

Said the Justice: "I have read Anne Frank's diary."

How this diary of a teen-age girl came to be written and saved is a story as dramatic as the diary itself. No one foresaw the tremendous impact the small book would have—not even her father, who had it published after Anne's death in a Nazi concentration camp.

*The Diary of Anne Frank* has now been published in 20 languages, including German, and has sold close to 5 million copies. Made into a play by Frances Goodrich and Albert Hackett, it won the Pulitzer Prize for Drama and, in the 1956–1957 season alone, was shown in 20 different countries to 2 million people. In 1959, the 20th Century Fox film won the Grand Prize of the International Catholic Film Bureau.

To understand this amazing response, it is necessary first to understand the girl who was Anne Frank.

When Hitler came to power, Otto Frank was a banker, living in Germany. He had married in 1925. In 1926, his first daughter, Margot, was born and three years later his second, Annelies Marie. She was usually called "Anne," sometimes "Tender One."

In the autumn of 1933, when Hitler was issuing one anti-Jewish decree after another, Otto Frank decided to immigrate to the hospitable Netherlands. He started a small firm in Amsterdam. Shortly before the outbreak of war, he took in a partner, Mr. Van Daan, a fellow refugee. Mostly they traded in spices. Trade was often slow. Once Otto Frank was forced to ask his small staff to accept a temporary cut in their modest wages. No one left. They all liked his warm personality. They admired his courage and the evident care he took to give his two girls a good education.

As a pupil, Anne was not particularly brilliant. Most people believed, with her parents, that Margot, her elder sister, was more promising. Anne was chiefly remarkable for the early interest she took in people. She was emotional and strong-willed; "a real problem child," her father once told me, "a great talker and fond of nice clothes." Life in town, where she was usually surrounded by a chattering crowd of girl friends, suited her exactly.

When the Nazis invaded the Netherlands in May 1940, the Franks were trapped. Earlier than most Jews in Amsterdam, Otto Frank realized that the time might come when he and his family would have to go into hiding. He decided to hide in his own office, which faced one of Amsterdam's tree-lined canals. A few derelict rooms on the upper floors, called the "Annexe," were secretly prepared to house both the Frank and the Van Daan families.

Early in July 1942, Margot Frank was called up for deportation, but she did not go. Straightaway, the Franks moved into their hiding place, and the Van Daans followed shortly afterward. Four months later they took into their cramped lodgings another Jew, a dentist.

They were eight hunted people. Any sound, any light might betray their presence. A tenuous link with the outside was provided by the radio and by four courageous members of Otto Frank's staff, two of them typists, who in secret brought food, magazines, books. The only other company they had was a cat.

While in hiding, Anne decided to continue a diary that her parents had given her on her thirteenth birthday. She described life in the Annexe, with all its inevitable tensions and quarrels. But she created first and foremost a wonderfully delicate record of adolescence, sketching with complete honesty a young girl's thoughts and feelings, her longing and loneliness. "I feel like a songbird whose wings have been brutally torn out and who is flying in utter darkness against the bars of its own cage," she wrote when she had been isolated from the outside world for nearly 16 months. Two months later she had filled every page of the diary, a small book bound in a tartan cloth, and one of the typists, Miep, gave her an ordinary exercise book. Later she used Margot's chemistry exercise book.

Her diary reveals the trust she puts in a wise father; her grief because, as she feels it, her mother does not understand her; the ecstasy of a first, rapturous kiss, exchanged with the Van Daans' 17-year-old son; finally, the flowering of a charmingly feminine personality, eager to face life with adult courage and mature self-insight.

On a slip of paper Anne wrote faked names that she intended to use in case of publication. For the time being the diary was her own secret, which she wanted to keep from everyone, especially from the grumpy dentist with whom she had to share her tiny bedroom. Her father allowed her to put her diaries in his briefcase.

He never read them until after her death.

On August 4, 1944, one German and four Dutch Nazi policemen suddenly stormed upstairs. (How the secret of the Annexe had been revealed is not known.) "Where are your money and jewels?" they shouted. Mrs. Frank and Mrs. Van Daan had some gold and jewelry. It was quickly discovered. Looking round for something to carry it in, one of the policemen noticed Otto Frank's briefcase. He emptied it onto the floor, barely giving a glance to the notebooks. Then the people of the Annexe were taken into arrest.

In the beginning of September, while the Allied armies under Eisenhower were rapidly approaching the

Netherlands, the Franks and Van Daans and the dentist were carried in cattle trucks to Auschwitz—the Nazi death camp in southern Poland. There the Nazis separated Otto Frank from his wife and daughters without giving them time to say farewell. Mrs. Frank, Anne and Margot were marched into the women's part of the camp, where Mrs. Frank died from exhaustion. The Van Daans and the dentist, too, lost their lives.

Anne proved to be a courageous leader of her small Auschwitz group. When there was nothing to eat, she dared to go to the kitchen to ask for food. She constantly told Margot never to give in. Once she passed hundreds of Hungarian Jewish children who were standing naked in freezing rain, waiting to be led to the gas chambers, unable to grasp the horrors inflicted upon them in the world of adults. "Oh, look, their eyes …" she whispered.

Later in the autumn, she and her sister were transported to another camp, Bergen-Belsen, between Berlin and Hamburg. A close friend saw her there: "cold and hungry, her head shaved and her skeleton-like form draped in the coarse, shapeless striped garb of the concentration camp." She was pitifully weak, her body racked by typhoid fever. She died in early March 1945, a few days after Margot. Both were buried in a mass grave.

In Auschwitz, Otto had managed somehow to stay alive. He was freed early in 1945 by the Russians, and in the summer he arrived back in liberated Amsterdam. A friend had told him that his wife had died, but he kept hoping that Anne and Margot would return. After six weeks of waiting, he met someone who had to tell him that both had perished. It was only then that Miep, his former typist, handed him Anne's diaries.

A week after the Frank family had been arrested, Miep had boldly returned to the Annexe. A heap of paper lay on the floor. Miep recognized Anne's handwriting and decided to keep the diary but not to read it. Had she read it, she would have found detailed information on the help she and other people had given the Frank family at the risk of their own lives, and she might well have decided to destroy the diary for reasons of safety.

It took Otto Frank many weeks to finish reading what his dead child had written. He broke down after every few pages. As his old mother was still alive—she had immigrated to Switzerland where other near relatives lived—he started copying the manuscript for her. He left out some passages that he felt were too intimate or that might hurt other people's feelings. The idea of publishing the diary did not enter his mind. He gave one typed copy to a close friend, who lent it to a professor of modern history. Much to Otto Frank's surprise, the professor devoted an article to it in a Dutch newspaper. His friends now urged Otto Frank to have Anne's diary published as she herself had wished: "I want to publish a book entitled *The Annexe* after the war. … My diary can serve this purpose." When Anne's father finally consented to publication, the manuscript was refused by two well-known Dutch publishers. A third decided to accept it, and he has sold more than 320,000 copies of the Netherlands edition.

Other editions followed—395,000 sold in Japan, a like number in England, 2,200,000 in the United States. Otto Frank began to receive hundreds of letters. One,

> Anne proved to be a courageous leader of her small Auschwitz group. When there was nothing to eat, she dared to go to the kitchen to ask for food.

from Italy, was addressed, "Otto Frank, father of Anne Frank, Amsterdam." A few people doubted the authenticity of the diary; most wrote to express their admiration and grief. Girls of Anne's age poured out their troubles: "Oh, Mr. Frank," wrote one American girl, "she is so much like me that sometimes I do not know where myself begins and Anne Frank ends." Numerous people sent small presents. Some exquisite dolls were made for him by Japanese girls. A Dutch sculptress presented him with a statue of Anne. On the birthdays of Anne and Margot, flowers arrived at his home anonymously.

So many letters poured in that Otto Frank was forced to retire from business. The care of his daughter's diary has become his passion, his mission in life. He now lives modestly in Switzerland. All royalties are devoted to humanitarian projects that, he feels, would have been approved by Anne. All letters are answered by him personally. Every day new ones sadly remind him of the losses he has suffered, but he feels that there is truth and consolation in what the headmistress of one of England's largest schools wrote to him: "It must be a source of deep joy to you—in all your sorrow—to know that Anne's brief life is, in the deepest sense, only just beginning."

The most remarkable response came from Germany. When the book's first printing of 4,500 copies came out in Germany in 1950, many booksellers were afraid to put it in their windows. Now sales of the German paperback edition total more than 750,000.

When the play opened in seven German cities simultaneously, no one knew how the audience would react. The drama progressed through its eight brief scenes. No "Nazis" were seen on the stage, but their ominous presence made itself felt every minute. Finally, at the end, Nazi jackboots were heard storming upstairs to raid the hiding place. At the end of the epilogue, only Anne's father was on stage, a lonely old man. Quietly he told how he received news that his wife and daughters had died. Picking up Anne's slim diary, he turned back the pages to find a certain passage, and as he found it, her young, confident voice was heard, saying, "In spite of everything, I still believe that people are really good at heart."

Packed audiences received Anne Frank's tragedy in silence heavy with remorse. In Dusseldorf people did not even go out during the intermission. "They sat in their seats as if afraid of the lights outside, ashamed to face each other," someone reported. The Dusseldorf producer, Kuno Epple, explained, "*Anne Frank* has succeeded because it enables the audience to come to grips with history, personally and without denunciation. We watch it as an indictment, in the most humble, pitiful terms, of inhumanity to fellow men. No one accuses us as Germans. We accuse ourselves."

For years Germany's postwar administrators toiled to make people feel the senseless and criminal nature of the Nazi regime. On the whole they failed. *The Diary of Anne Frank* succeeded. The play has now been presented in 93 West German and 34 East German cities and has been seen by some 3 million Germans. Leading actors have received dozens of letters. "I was a good Nazi," a typical letter read, "but I never knew what it meant until the other night." German schoolchildren sent Otto Frank letters signed by entire classes, telling

him that Anne's diary had opened their eyes to the viciousness of racial persecution.

In West Berlin an Anne Frank Home was opened, devoted to social work for young people. The people of Berlin had chosen her name "to symbolize the spirit of racial and social tolerance." Elsewhere in Germany, an organization was set up, named after her, to combat the remaining vestiges of anti-Semitism. In Vienna money was collected for the Anne Frank forest, now being planted in Israel.

In March 1957, a Hamburg student suggested that flowers should be laid on the mass graves of Bergen-Belsen, where Anne Frank had found her last resting place. More than 2,000 young people eagerly

> # Every day Otto Frank gets letters. They remind him of his losses, but also bring consolation and hope. One woman wrote that "Anne's brief life is, in the deepest sense, just beginning."

answered his appeal. Hundreds pedaled on bikes 80 miles in lashing rain. Standing in front of one of the mass graves, a 17-year-old schoolgirl expressed what all felt: "Anne Frank was younger than we are when her life was so horribly ended. She had to die because others had decided to destroy her race. Never again among our people must such a diseased and inhuman hatred arise."

Anne's brief life is, indeed, only beginning. She carries a message of courage and tolerance all over the world. She lives after death. ∎

# THE GIVER WAS The Gift

### By Elizabeth Westfall Flynn
~

When I was a kid, I worshipped my big brother, Kemper. He was a loyal friend, someone who always faced down a bully, a protector of his three sisters. And he was cool; he did exciting things. When my parents went out of town, he had parties so big it looked like the world had been invited. Everybody loved him—but trouble knew where to find him, too.

In 1967, he joined the Marines and fought in Vietnam. By the tender age of 20, he had witnessed the decimation of his platoon.

When he finally came home, he was different. Quiet, not interested in the homecoming party my parents wanted to throw for him. Not even excited about the '69 VW Bug they gave him tied up in a bow. He spent the next few years of his life trying to adjust.

But he never did. In 1977, he killed himself, leaving a note asking for forgiveness. When his wallet was returned to us, it reeked of exhaust fumes. His death tore my family apart. My parents divorced, and my heart was broken.

Then, on a brisk, sunny day a week before Christmas last year, I was out shopping and called home from my car to check on my son. "Mom, some woman phoned and said she was hired by the court to find you. It has to do with your brother."

An old forgotten bank account? I wondered. I called her immediately and was connected with a woman who said she was a confidential intermediary. "I have reason to believe," she said, "you are the biological relative of a female born October 21, 1965, who is seeking medical information. Were you aware your brother fathered a child in 1965? Hello?" I was so shocked I couldn't respond.

My brother's girlfriend had become pregnant when they were in high school, and neither Kemper nor my parents ever told anyone. Now his daughter was looking for us. I sat in the car with my foot on the brake and just cried.

Bonnie Jean Phoenix had a happy childhood. Her parents were loving and nurturing—exactly the kind of adoptive parents Kemper and his frightened girlfriend would have hoped for. But throughout her life, Bonnie had a feeling of disconnectedness. At age 34, she decided it was time to solve the mystery of her origin, and she began the search. It took her three years.

The day she walked into my mother's house, I was stunned. Here was a perfect stranger who was the image of my brother—his nose, his mouth, his blue-green eyes. She looked like an angel standing in the sunlit hallway. *He sent her to us,* I thought, *to love in his place.*

I introduced myself, and before I knew it, her arms were around me. She brought a box full of pictures of herself as a child—playing with a pet, swinging in a hammock. A child who always stood up for others—a cheery little girl, her face beaming.

In the days and weeks after meeting Bonnie, I realized a weight was beginning to lift. It was the anger I'd had for years and never wanted to admit. I was angry at my brother for committing suicide. My parents' marriage collapsed, and my sisters and I worried that life's battles might be too much for our own sons. For the next 25 years, my brother's death and the manner of it haunted us all.

Then Bonnie found us. She is so much like him. She's reminded me of what a good guy he was. She made me believe in happy endings again. She made me forgive him. ∎

ILLUSTRATION BY LEIGH WELLS

# Alone in a Runaway Balloon

Alex Nicholos wanted to help launch a hot-air balloon. Then a series of bizarre events sent him on the ride of his life.

By
Per Ola
and
Emily
D'Aulaire

Eleven-year-old Alex Nicholos was excited. Not only was it a sparkling winter morning that Sunday, January 7, 1990, in Colorado Springs—it was also the day that Alex, his 9-year-old sister and their parents were going to help their friend Tex Houston launch his hot-air balloon.

A half-mile away, Dave Hollenbaugh, 60, rubbed the sleep from his eyes. He had been fighting the flu for weeks and felt miserable. He wanted to stay in bed, but he,

ILLUSTRATION BY PAUL DEGEN

too, had promised to help Houston with his balloon, aptly named The Yellow Rose of Tex's.

Hollenbaugh and the Nicholos family arrived at the launch field shortly after sunrise. Houston, a portly, genial man, was already there, along with five other balloonists and their crews.

Alex and his father, George Nicholos, hauled on the crown line attached to the top of the balloon's 75-foot-high envelope. The boy's mother, Linda, and sister, Stephanie, held open the mouth of the balloon for the inflation process. Houston climbed into the wicker basket and lit the powerful propane burner to heat the air inside the balloon. Two other ground-crew members, Shawn Tayloe and Debbie Prosise, held the basket down. Before long The Yellow Rose towered as high as an eight-story building. Alex all but danced with excitement. Anything mechanical fascinated him, especially things that flew.

His curiosity about how things work was important, because Alex had a minor brain dysfunction called attention deficit disorder (ADD). As a result, though bright, the fifth-grader was a slow book-learner. He did best when things were demonstrated. Typical of ADD children, Alex was impulsive, easily distracted, and his moods and emotions could swing widely.

Hollenbaugh was the opposite: calm, methodical, unemotional. An Air Force pilot for 24 years, he had served in Vietnam. In 1973, he suffered decompression sickness in a plane that lost its pressurization system. Even though he fully recovered, he was eliminated from flight status. Hollenbaugh retired from the military and later earned his balloon pilot's license and qualified as an instructor.

Now, with The Yellow Rose poised for flight, Hollenbaugh heard Houston call out to Alex, "Hey, want a ride?" The delighted boy clambered into the wicker basket and donned a crash helmet. Moments later, the bright yellow balloon lifted off into the cobalt sky, following the breeze and five other balloons.

George, Linda and Stephanie climbed into the rear seat of Houston's van. Shawn took the wheel. Debbie sat in the center seat, map in hand, with Hollenbaugh to her right, where he could keep the balloon in sight through the windshield and the side window. He held a CB microphone, ready, if the need arose, to talk with Houston.

Watching his family grow smaller beneath him, Alex gasped in awe. Soon he began to bombard Houston with questions: "How do you heat the balloon? How does the radio work? What are you doing now?"

Houston answered every question carefully. Alex watched as Houston pulled the lanyard attached to the burner valve, releasing a roar of propane flame into the mouth of the balloon to make it rise after each slight "downhill" coast.

Between "burns," Houston pointed out the flight instruments: fuel gauges; the variometer that showed whether the balloon was rising or falling, and how fast; a temperature gauge that indicated when it was time to turn the burner on or off. What fascinated Alex most was the CB radio.

A half-hour into the flight, Houston noticed the breeze increasing. The other balloons, two miles ahead, had begun their descent. He spotted a flat area, the last suitable site before a wooded expanse called the Black Forest, and radioed Hollenbaugh that he planned to land.

"Squat down," Houston warned Alex. "We may be in for a bumpy landing." Alex hunkered low, holding on to the inside wall of the basket and closing his eyes. Then, unexpectedly, he heard the throaty roar of the burner and felt the balloon rise abruptly.

Houston had aborted the landing. Below the basket, directly in its line of travel, was a barbed-wire fence. Ahead of that, blocking their route, was an electrical power line.

In the chase vehicle, Hollenbaugh was becoming concerned. The winds had picked up to a brisk 15 miles per hour. *Why hadn't Houston set the balloon down?* he wondered. He switched on the CB. "Yellow Rose, what are your intentions?"

"I see a flat space on the far side of the forest," Houston replied. "I'll land there."

Twenty feet from the snow-covered ground, the balloon's basket disappeared from Hollenbaugh's view as it went behind a knoll. The upper half of the balloon tilted forward, an indication that the craft had hit and was dragging. Then the balloon straightened itself and shot skyward. *Tex really botched that one,* Hollenbaugh thought.

The moment The Yellow Rose touched down, the basket pitched forward so sharply that its upper edge plowed into the snow. The result was a sudden jolting motion that threw Houston forward, catapulting him out of the basket. He grabbed for Alex but missed.

Crouched in a corner of the basket with his eyes still closed, Alex didn't realize what was happening at first. "Boy, that was a close one," he said, looking around. But Tex Houston was gone!

"There's Tex!" Shawn shouted. "He's down!" Hollenbaugh looked toward the site of the aborted landing. Houston was limping over the rise, waving his arms. *Where was Alex?* Just then the radio crackled to life with Alex's high-pitched, frightened voice. "Help me," Alex pleaded. "I'm scared!" Hollenbaugh looked up at the balloon racing silently through the sky. *The boy is up there alone!*

Houston, in emotional shock, reached the van. "I'm sorry," he kept muttering. "I'm so sorry."

Alex's mother and sister began sobbing, and his father tried to comfort them, fighting back his own terror. Hollenbaugh knew he had to keep himself and everyone else calm. He reached for the radio. "It's all right, Alex," he assured the frightened youngster. "You're the pilot now, and I'm going to teach you how to land the balloon."

*What's the minimum the boy needs to know to fly the balloon?* Hollenbaugh knew that if he overloaded Alex with information, the boy would not be able to follow instructions. Hollenbaugh told Alex how to work the blast valve that shoots a 12-foot flame into the balloon's envelope. He decided not to mention the vent line, which also controls altitude by temporarily dumping hot air. Alex might confuse it with the rip line, which if pulled, could send the balloon plummeting. Alex would need the rip line when he landed, though, so Hollenbaugh told him where it was and not to touch it yet.

From the speeding van, Hollenbaugh couldn't tell whether The Yellow Rose was going up or down, so he explained to Alex how to read the variometer. "What's the needle doing now?" Hollenbaugh asked repeatedly.

Alex felt enormous relief when he heard the man's quiet voice over the CB. He sounded so reassuring, so personal, that it was more like talking to a friend than to a stranger. *He doesn't sound worried*, Alex thought. *Maybe I'll be okay.*

But whenever the balloon sank, the boy would panic. "I'm falling!" he'd yell into the mike. "What if I crash?" Then he'd pull the lanyard that turned on the burner to propel the balloon skyward.

Hollenbaugh worried that Alex would add too much heat and send The Yellow Rose too high, where strong winds could quickly carry the boy beyond CB-radio range. If that happened, Alex would have no hope. "We won't let you fall, I promise," Hollenbaugh radioed Alex. "Please don't use the burner until I tell you."

Once he realized that he could follow Hollenbaugh's instructions, Alex felt more secure. He liked reading the instruments and reporting back. *I really can fly this thing*, Alex told himself proudly.

The chase van soon met up with a car carrying Rollie Elkins, one of the other balloonists who had landed earlier. Elkins had been Houston's instructor and knew The Yellow Rose intimately. He jumped in the van to assist Hollenbaugh.

The terrain was more open now, range land with fewer trees and rocks. "Alex," Hollenbaugh spoke firmly into the radio. "I need you to bring the balloon down closer to the ground so I can help you land."

Hollenbaugh told Alex how to handle the burns. "Now, burn—one, two ... stop. You're doing fine, Alex. Burn—one, two. ..." Slowly, smoothly, The Yellow Rose descended from 2,000 to 200 feet, then sailed majestically 90 feet above a farmhouse, just clearing a power line.

The balloon crossed the road in front of them at 50 feet. "Alex, reach up and grab the rip line I told you about, sit on the bottom of the basket and pull, pull, pull. ..."

The basket hit the ground, bounced once, dragged along the ground a short distance, then settled on its side, the envelope collapsing. When all was still, the uninjured boy was found pulling on the rope, making certain that The Yellow Rose was grounded for good. Amazingly, after 90 minutes alone in the air, covering some 35 miles, the fifth-grader had brought the balloon down in a textbook high-wind landing.

Through the ordeal, Hollenbaugh's voice had been so easy-going that Alex never fully realized the danger he faced. When his parents swept him in their arms, crying, he was surprised. "Gee, I'm sorry I got everybody so frightened," he said.

Hollenbaugh sat in the van, unable to move. Then he broke down. "Thank you, God, oh, thank you," he murmured, tears streaming down his face.

> # Where was Alex? Just then the radio crackled to life with Alex's high-pitched, frightened voice. "Help me," Alex pleaded. "I'm scared!"

When Linda Nicholos brought Alex over to thank Hollenbaugh, the boy stared at the man as if perplexed. "You sounded a lot younger," Alex said.

Hollenbaugh smiled wanly. "Believe me, Alex, before we started all this, I was."

The next day in school Alex's solo ballooning feat was announced on the intercom, and all his teachers praised his courage. He proudly displayed the balloon pilot's wings that Tex Houston had taken off his own chest and given to him.

"I got through that balloon ride," Alex says. "Now I can get through anything."

The National Aeronautic Association awarded Hollenbaugh its Certificate of Honor for safety. He is the first balloonist to receive it for this achievement. "It was the longest, toughest flight of my life," Hollenbaugh says, "and I never left the ground." ∎

# Where Brought

## As a child Lauralee was dependent on welfare and homeless shelters. But she found comfort in her books—and the Hobbits.

*By Suzanne Chazin*

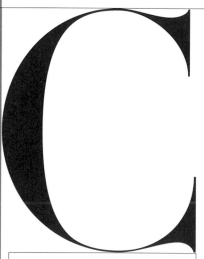

Cold fluorescent lights flickered to life as the 9-year-old girl roused herself from her metal cot and fumbled for her glasses. In the shadowless glare of the room, shabby women stumbled about, cursing and muttering to themselves. It was 6 a.m. and still dark outside. Beyond the curtainless windows of the Salvation Army homeless shelter in Santa Barbara, Calif., a halo of streetlights and a cool Pacific Ocean wind heralded the start of another day.

Lauralee Summer settled her bare feet on the concrete floor and slowly began to dress. Everyone had to check out of the shelter by 7:30 a.m. No one was allowed back until 5:30 that evening.

"Hurry along, dear," urged the soft voice of her mother, Elizabeth, from the cot next to hers. "You want to be on time for school."

*School.* The word once conjured up pleasant thoughts for Lauralee. That was no longer so.

ILLUSTRATION BY MICHELLE CHANG

# LOVE
# Lauralee

Lauralee could not concentrate enough to read in the shelter, and she couldn't learn at school. For her, school meant sitting in a fourth-grade classroom with children who were happy and had homes. She felt different, isolated.

Raised solely by her mother, Lauralee knew nothing but a life dependent on welfare, food stamps and the kindness of family and strangers all over the country. Her impulsive mother, always brimming with wanderlust, never seemed able to settle in one place. Lauralee had already moved at least eight times to three states. She was fed up.

"I'm not going to school," she declared.

When her mother grimaced, Lauralee screamed the words again, pounding the wall with her fists. "I hate you. I hate this place. And I hate school. I'm not going."

More than anything, 45-year-old Elizabeth wanted Lauralee to get an education. Yet during those dreary winter days of 1986, both mother and daughter began to question whether that was possible.

**As a small child, Lauralee didn't realize she lacked anything.** Her mother was a natural teacher who infused much joy and wonder into all their hardships. Together they studied the stars. They made castles out of oatmeal cartons.

Even when Lauralee grew older, she didn't realize that one reason they spent evenings sprawled out on a shag carpet reading Shakespeare's *A Midsummer Night's Dream* was that they couldn't afford television.

*I barrage my mother with questions about the fairies, about Puck. She answers patiently in a way that I will understand. She doesn't see Shakespeare's play as a text that can only be understood and analyzed by literary critics. She boldly believes that a 6-year-old can be a valid critic.* *

The little girl didn't know that they sometimes made biscuits for dinner because that was all they had left from their food-stamp money at the end of the month. She did not realize the reason they took long walks was that they didn't have a car.

Because of her mother's ingenuity, Lauralee saw these expeditions on foot as adventures. Elizabeth had time to teach her the varieties of plants in a garden, time to make up stories and to sing songs. It was a period of innocence and joy.

As she grew older, Lauralee became acutely aware of a dichotomy in her life. For all her mother's ability to read serious books, she found it hard to make some decisions. Especially small ones—like what to eat for dinner or when to catch a bus.

The big decisions she often made impulsively—like selling their possessions and moving on the vague notion that elsewhere jobs were more plentiful, the climate was more temperate and the cost of living lower.

*\*This and other italicized passages are drawn from Lauralee's writings.*

To escape the constant turmoil of her life, Lauralee threw herself into books. It wasn't just escape she sought. The stories had a structure that seemed lacking in her own life. One of her favorites was J.R.R. Tolkien's *The Hobbit*, a tale of mythical creatures on a fantastical journey. She read it so many times, she committed the first page to memory.

Her vagabond existence allowed for little space or privacy. In the midst of dinginess and chaos, her refuge was the bathtub. And it was there, turning pages grown damp with steam, that she closed off the outside world and filled her mind with the images conjured up from lines of print.

Lost in a story, she no longer noticed the bathroom's loose tiles, leaky faucets or peeling plaster. There were only Hobbits and heroes and wondrous adventures.

**But the world outside Lauralee's books intruded harshly** on a regular basis. Once, during a visit to the welfare office, her mother tried to explain a problem about food stamps to a caseworker, who smiled at her condescendingly.

Lauralee stared at the floor, embarrassment welling up inside her. To her dismay, she realized that she was feeling this way more and more.

When Elizabeth Summer was grieving over her own mother's death, she decided that life for her and her daughter would be better in California. That was when they left Oregon for Santa Barbara.

Something changed in Lauralee after this move. The little girl who loved Shakespeare and long walks and biscuits by the stove no longer made up stories.

After living in two California shelters, Lauralee had begun to see the world in a harsh new light. There were the haves and the have-nots.

*I don't go to school during sunny California days. I shoplift with a friend. I know this is wrong, but I like the pretty clothes, and I like my friend. I wear dreamy armfuls of plastic and metallic bracelets that girls my age collect.*

Lauralee would jingle the bracelets in front of her mother and lie about where she got them. Elizabeth suspected nothing until the afternoon Lauralee and her friend were caught shoplifting jackets. The Santa Barbara police summoned their mothers.

The two arrived together. The other girl's mother immediately began screaming at her daughter. Elizabeth, however, didn't speak at first. She gave Lauralee only a disappointed look behind her huge glasses.

Lauralee's heart sank. She'd robbed her mother of the one thing she had always cherished—her faith in people, especially her daughter. She never shoplifted again. But Lauralee had begun to realize that as much as she loved her mother, Elizabeth Summer's eccentric behavior and chaotic lifestyle were taking their toll.

In frustration, Lauralee would taunt her mother: "You can't keep a job." Afterward, instead of feeling better for her outbursts, she felt worse. She wanted to love her mother, the nurturer of her soul, but how could she do that when their lives were in constant turmoil?

For her part, Elizabeth, an eternal optimist, recognized how unhappy her daughter was and decided to move back to Oregon.

**They lived in Oregon for a time** with Elizabeth's sister Jane; her husband, Ron; and their six children. It was a simple home, but 10-year-old Lauralee was in awe. There were always eggs and milk in the refrigerator and clean clothes neatly folded in the closets. Every coat had a hook, every mitten a match. Meals were planned and prepared in advance.

Aunt Jane, in turn, required the same discipline in all the children. A school secretary, she expected Lauralee to attend class every day, and each Sunday she took the children to church.

Lauralee joined the church youth group. There she heard the pastor speak about forgiveness and loving others in spite of their faults. Lauralee had noted how Aunt Jane never berated or judged her mother no matter how eccentric her actions sometimes seemed. She and Uncle Ron opened up their home unquestioningly to them.

When Lauralee asked why, Aunt Jane replied simply, "She is my sister. You are my niece. She is different than I am, but that doesn't mean I love her less."

Something clicked inside the girl. She began to let go of the anger that had built up during the time they were homeless in California. Her mother, she began to realize, was doing her best.

Lauralee's renewed appreciation of Elizabeth did not extend to school, however. In the seventh grade, Lauralee again dropped out, bored with junior high and angry at a teacher's accusations that an essay she had labored so hard over was too sophisticated to be her own work.

Elizabeth was still convinced that her little flower would bloom if just given the chance. Lauralee, she decided needed someplace with good schools, cultural activities and plenty of colleges nearby. She studied a map of the United States.

"We're moving to Boston," she announced suddenly to Lauralee one hot summer day.

**They arrived not knowing a soul,** most of their money spent on the trip. At a city welfare office, a caseworker assigned them two cots at a huge red-brick homeless shelter miles from the center of Boston. The Summers left the shelter after finding alternative housing, but Elizabeth

eventually decided it was best to put her daughter in a foster home until she could find a suitable place for both of them to stay.

Although there were four frantic dogs and six other foster children, the home was far from disorderly. Every day had a busy schedule filled with expectations and activities. All the children went to school. Dishes and coats had a place; beds were made. Each child had daily chores.

Lauralee greeted it all with enthusiasm. The change gave her some of the structure she was hungering for. Her dark mood about school lifted.

By the time Lauralee reached ninth grade, Elizabeth had found a small apartment in Quincy, Mass., for the two of them and took her daughter out of foster care.

> # Lauralee quit school, bored with seventh grade and angry at a teacher who said an essay she wrote was too sophisticated to be her own work.

Lauralee was determined once and for all to be the perfect student. She got involved with many after-school projects.

But the demands of her hectic school schedule began to take their toll. Lauralee never got enough sleep. Dark circles began to appear under her eyes, and her impish cheeks lost their luster. By the late fall of her sophomore year at Quincy High, she was burning out.

Charles MacLaughlin, director of Quincy High School's Heritage Program, an alternative-learning curriculum, was sitting in his office one day when Lauralee's English teacher came to his door. "We're going to lose this girl if we don't do something."

A fatherly man known to his students as Mr. Mac, MacLaughlin had heard about Lauralee's rootless life in shelters, foster homes and shabby apartments. Concerned, he agreed to talk to her and invited Lauralee to his office.

MacLaughlin had worked with scores of directionless teens. But he was unprepared for the young woman who walked through his door. What really floored him was the answer she gave to a question he routinely asked all the students: "What do you like to do?"

"Running," Lauralee began. "But most of all, I like to read."

MacLaughlin straightened. Not many of the kids he saw listed reading as a favorite activity.

"What kind of stuff?" he asked nonchalantly. He was stunned when Lauralee casually reeled off a long list of everything from Shakespeare to current teen fare.

Her teacher was right, he thought. They couldn't lose this girl. He designed a school program more suited to her intellect and needs. Hearing from teachers how patient she was and how easily she gave of herself to help others, he suggested that she teach reading to younger children.

The strategy worked. Lauralee began to blossom. Her grades improved. On a lark, a friend suggested they both try out for the wrestling team. Lauralee decided to give it a try, though she was only five-foot-four and 115 pounds. The friend chickened out, but Lauralee was hooked. It gave her a sense of belonging she'd so often missed.

**In December 1993, when Lauralee was a senior** MacLaughlin encouraged her to apply for a religion and literature course taught at night by the Harvard Extension program, a curriculum available to high school students in the Boston area.

Just before the Christmas break, one of the instructors took Lauralee aside and asked which colleges she was planning to apply to. When the teenager told her, the teacher asked, "Why haven't you considered Harvard?"

Lauralee stared at her in surprise.

*There's a lot that goes into a person's life and its direction. There's a lot that's determined by chance and divine providence—if you want to call it that—and we don't always understand the mysterious boosts we get from being in the right place, at the right time.*

After talking the matter over with Mr. Mac, Lauralee decided to apply. With the application deadline just days away, she holed up for a weekend in the bedroom of her mother's drab apartment, spending long hours filling out all the forms and crafting her essay.

Four months later, a thick envelope arrived in the mail from Harvard. She opened it with shaking hands: "I am delighted to inform you ..."

"I always knew you were special," Elizabeth told her daughter, hugging her.

At Harvard, Lauralee began to make that specialness known. She tried out for Harvard's varsity wrestling team and became its first woman member.

Lauralee tackled her studies in the same determined way, earning high grades throughout her four years and a degree in children's studies.

**On one sunny afternoon in June 1998,** a round, eager face peeked out from a line of Harvard graduates dressed in black caps and gowns. Lauralee Summer was about to receive her diploma.

> A teacher asked which colleges she planned to apply to. Lauralee told her and was surprised when the woman said, "Why haven't you considered Harvard?"

The 21-year-old's eyes nervously scanned the audience. As Lauralee stood in line to receive her diploma, she wondered if her mother, never very punctual, might miss her graduation.

The young woman tried to suppress the memories that popped into her head of other disappointments: the missed buses, the late dinners, the times she'd expected her mother to be somewhere and she wasn't.

Lauralee's name was called. Distractedly she stepped onto the platform and accepted her diploma. When the ceremony was over, she hoisted herself atop a low-lying brick wall to scan the crowd one more time. All around, elegantly dressed families doted on their children and snapped pictures.

As she was walking past a table where families had gathered to enjoy the graduation's buffet feast, a soft voice called her name. She turned, and there stood her mother, a Quincy High School Wrestling team baseball cap on her head, a peasant dress covering her small frame, smiling triumphantly.

"Did you see me get my diploma?" Lauralee asked, hugging her mother and holding up her leather-bound bachelor's degree.

"I got here just in time," Elizabeth said. "I always knew you could do it." She gave her daughter a tight squeeze. "I'm so happy."

*My little leap became a glorious Peter Pan-like adventure that gave me access to education, privilege and academic knowledge that was once a Never-Never Land for me.*

*It wasn't all me; it was my mother's fanciful whims, her intense care and guidance, her way of engaging my mind in thinking, in education, in reading. Love brought me here.* ∎

# LIFE'S LIKE THAT

**AS THE SON** of a college professor and a professor myself, I hoped my sons would go to college. But after our oldest found that the courses he wanted to take at the university were full, he got discouraged. I went to the registrar. I'd heard he was a stickler for rules, so I was floored when the man asked, "What classes would he like?" and took care of the problem on his computer.

Seeing my surprise, he explained that years before, he was in the same situation as my son. He'd met a professor who took him to the enrollment lines and got him into every class he wanted. "That man was your father. By any chance, is he still alive?"

I nodded. He smiled. "Good," he said. "Tell him we're even."

-THOMAS O. MORGAN, OVIEDO, FLA.

**SINCE MY 16-YEAR-OLD SON** recently received a prepaid cell phone as a gift, I've asked him to use it to call home if he's out past his curfew. One Saturday while waiting up for him, I dozed off in front of the TV. Later, I woke to realize that there was no sign of him and no call.

Irate, I punched in his number. When he answered, I demanded, "Where are you, and why haven't you bothered to phone?"

"Dad," he sleepily replied, "I'm upstairs in bed. I've been home for an hour."

-DON JENTLESON, DAYTON, OHIO

**WHEN THE ICE MAKER** in our new refrigerator broke, my husband dropped by the store to arrange for repairs. Because the sun was bright, my husband's eyes hadn't adjusted to the dim light inside in time to see a woman sitting on the floor examining carpet samples.

He stepped on her leg, and she screamed, causing him to jump into a display of fireplace tools that went crashing in every direction. Unnerved, my husband stumbled over to the service desk, and as he went to rest his hands on the counter, he flipped over a bowl full of marbles, scattering them everywhere.

After taking a deep breath to calm himself, he announced to the wide-eyed woman working there, "My refrigerator doesn't work."

"I don't doubt it," she replied.

-MARLENE RITTER, BOULDER, COLO.

After taking a tour of a winery in New Jersey, our group waited patiently to get to the wine-tasting counter. That was not easy, since a man ahead of us was hogging the samples as well as the attention of the salesperson.

Finally it seemed that he was winding down, as he asked the salesperson, "What should I take back to my snobby friends in California?" That's when my wife whispered to me, "How about the bus?"

-GUY GREEN, LEHIGHTON, PA.

**MY SISTER'S** lack of sports knowledge recently became evident when we attended a pro-hockey game. After one of the home players scored, the crowd screamed and the monitors around the rink flashed, "G O A L."

After cheering wildly, my sister turned and asked, "Who's Al?"

-KAREN KELLY, BENSALEM, PA.

# Rearing Children In Samoa

*By Margaret Mead*

~

In this landmark report, the world's most renowned anthropologist showed how children in Samoa grow differently than those in America. Mead, flanked by Samoans in this photo, lived among them.

hen I picked a tiny island in American Samoa and set out to study adolescent children in that primitive community, I asked myself this question: Are Samoan children torn by the conflicts, baffled by the spiritual doubts and tormented by the vague ambitions that are always considered an unavoidable element in the lives of American children of the same difficult age?

The answer, I found, was emphatically no. The period of adolescence was unstressed. Girls changed without vexation from little girls whose main business was baby-tending to big girls who could be trusted with longer and more difficult tasks. No conflicts with their parents, no confusion about sex vexed their souls. Their development was smooth, untroubled, unstressed. What is there in South Sea society that makes the difference?

The first big difference is in the family. Our typical family—father, mother and children—is hardly ever found in Samoa. The Samoans live in great households of ten to 20 people—father and mother, aunts, uncles, grandparents, relatives-in-law, cousins—all housed in a cluster of round open houses, with high thatched roofs, no walls and no privacy. In such families there is no youngest child, not for long. Some sister or aunt or cousin will have a baby in the next few months. There is no only child, the spoiled indulged pet of a family of adults. Similarly, the sharp division between parents and children vanishes. A family is just a long series of people of different ages, all somehow related to one another, grading down from the grandfather to the new baby.

The importance and prestige of the real father and mother are shared and diminished by the presence of a lot of other grown-up people. Furthermore, the mother takes very little care of her own babies after they are about six months old. At that age they are handed over to children of six and seven, who trundle them about everywhere, astride their hips. As often as not, it isn't mother who dries the baby's tears, nor father who spanks the little mischief makers. And so the setting for parent fixations vanishes; the relationship between Samoan parents and children is too casual to foster such attitudes.

In this the advantages are surely on the side of Samoa. In our civilization, the self-conscious parent is forever sheltering the child—from bad grammar, from the measles, from casual associates. The American parent needs to remember always that wholesome social intercourse is essential to the healthy development of a child.

Life and death and sex are no mysteries to the growing child in Samoa. The horror, the shock, the nauseated recoil of our protected, unsophisticated children is unknown. In Samoa, little toddlers peep under the midwife's arm at birth, hover about the group preparing a corpse, and make an evening game of spying upon wandering lovers. The amatory arts are freely discussed, and the whole village stands ready to mock the inept lover. Any untimely, precocious participation in adult affairs is the most heinous of crimes, but this applies to actions, not to knowledge. Samoan children are not confused by false teaching. Hence they grow up with the best equipment in the world against shock—experience.

> To the Samoan, sex is an art, a play to be learned with care and practiced with discretion. These are not love affairs as we conceive of them.

In this armoring of the children's nerves, quite as important a factor as the actual experience is the attitude of the parents. The grown people regard the whole course of human life simply. They consider sex as natural, birth as unexceptional. The spectator children are surrounded by their parents' uncomplicated attitudes. The facts of life, learned young enough, do not stagger nor particularly interest the young child, but the affective tone that surrounds the moment may permanently influence this whole attitude.

Our society is organized upon the basis of rewards for the swift, the precocious. Samoa distrusts all precocity. The child who boasts of having performed some adult task is not praised. Instead he is roundly berated at home, and his conduct is publicly deprecated. Our adolescent children are met upon all sides by demands that they choose between religious faiths, between careers, between political allegiances. Samoan children are told to get up early in the morning, keep their mouths shut, listen attentively and wait till they have more judgment. The danger in the Samoan method, of course, is that it can blunt the ambitions and blur the spontaneity of gifted children. On the other hand, backward children are greatly helped. Inferiority complexes do not flourish in such an atmosphere.

At about 16 or 17 the girl has passed through the most marked period of adolescence and is ready for a way of life that holds no mystery for her. Her ambition is simple: She wishes as a girl to have as many affairs and as few responsibilities as possible; then to marry near home and have many children.

Her love affairs begin. Although surrounded by the trappings that seem to us most romantic—moonlight, palm trees, the rhythmic beat of the surf, white with "coral milk," the soft perfume of the frangipani blossoms, low-voiced protestations of love and flowery invocations of the stars and moon—these affairs are not love affairs as we conceive of them. Samoan amours are more like the petting conventions of our younger generation.

Comeliness and technique are the two most important requisites. Friendship, appreciation of personality, passionate love with its strong feelings of fidelity and chivalry—all are lacking. To the Samoan, sex is an art, a play to be learned with care and practiced with discretion. The emphasis is all upon the proper note of casualness, upon the fleeting hour.

Later, the Samoan girl is to enter upon a marriage of convenience arranged by her parents. Should she learn the meaning of a strong attachment to one person, a conflict might ensue. But she does not. She meets young men as lovers for brief butterfly affairs. And she marries, not to satisfy vague, undefined desires, but because she is a little weary of the love that flits so lightly among the palm trees and wants the social position of a married woman and children of her own.

The experience and perfection of sex knowledge in Samoa makes for happiness, but the absence of strong personal ties can only be deplored. The indiscriminate lovemaking and its necessary suppression of any genuine emotion lead to a disregard of the importance of personal relations. We can appreciate, as the Samoans cannot, the value of personal relations.

We could not reproduce the Samoan conditions if we would. Our complicated society, which is coming to realize personality as a value and cherish individuality of thought, demands higher prices than are ever paid by the graceful young Samoans in their shady, peaceful villages. And these prices our youth have to pay. Their young days can never be as untroubled, as unpoignant as the days of the Samoans. ∎

# LIFE IN THESE UNITED STATES

**MY MOTHER** is a cleaning fanatic. One Saturday she told me and my brother to get down to the playroom and straighten it up. We had had a party there the previous evening, and she was none too happy about the mess.

As she watched us work, it was clear Mom was completely dissatisfied with our cleaning efforts, and she let us know it.

Finally my brother, exasperated with having to do it all over, reached for a broom and asked, "Can I use this or are you planning to go somewhere?"

-MARK BERMAN, LOS ANGELES, CALIF.

**OUR NEIGHBOR** loaned my husband his old chain saw to trim some tree branches. Unfortunately, the engine burned out while my husband was using it. Not wanting to return a broken piece of equipment, he bought a new saw to replace it.

When I offered it to our neighbor, he thanked me but said, "Keep it. I'll borrow it when I need it."

I was turning away when his eyes lit up. "Hey," he asked, "want to borrow my car?"

-PATRICIA A. BROPHY, HERNDON, VA.

**EVEN THOUGH** he's in his 30s, my husband still has a baby face. I didn't think I was sensitive to comments about his looking younger until one night when we were out with some college-age friends. After we ordered drinks, the waitress asked my husband for his ID. "Don't you want to see my ID, too?" I asked indignantly.

"Ma'am," she coolly replied, "you ordered a Coke."

-BEVERLY GALLAGHER, CARMEL, IND.

# *Unforgettable* BING

The two legends shared a great friendship that survived being rivals, working together for 30 years. Here, Bob Hope thanks his buddy for the memories of a lifetime.

# Crosby

*By Bob Hope*

It's funny how many times the most lasting friendships of our lives begin in a moment so incidental we scarcely recall it. Bing Crosby and I shook hands outside the Friars Club on 48th Street in New York one autumn day back in 1932. He was already a recording star and had one of the most popular radio shows in the country. I was a comedian fresh out of vaudeville and nibbling at a Broadway career.

Two months later I was emceeing in a variety show at New York's Capitol Theater, and Crosby was the lead singer. It was the first time our names appeared together on a marquee. Across from the theater there happened to be a watering hole in which Bing and I repaired each evening between shows. We started kidding each other, then developing little bits to work into the show. The crowd in the bar loved it. Who can define what the chemistry was between the easygoing crooner from Tacoma via Spokane and the erstwhile boxer and vaudeville hoofer from England via Cleveland? It was just there.

On our respective radio shows during the 1930s, we both fostered the "Hope-Crosby Feud." He took potshots at my nose ("like a bicycle seat"), my golf and even my jokes. I fired back at "Ol' Dad," the aging star, ribbing him about everything from his "groaning" to his rapidly thinning hair and jug ears.

One night he walked on, unexpected, during my radio show. "Tell me, Bing," I said, "with so much hot air and those ears, why don't you take off?" He replied, chuckling, "The downdraft from your nose prevents it."

Bing could kid around about those very things that made other stars founder in a morass of vanity. He once wrote regarding my incessant razzing over the hairpiece Paramount made him wear in his films: "Robert Hope, of the non-classic profile and the unlissome midsection, is sometimes goaded by a knowledge of his own lack of physical charms into referring to me as skin head. I don't have to specify what it means. It's generally known that for screen purposes I wear a device the trade calls a scalp doily."

By the time I got to Hollywood and signed with Paramount, Crosby had already made his mark in movies. By then, too, ol' Cros was also a little mad about horses, though the ones he bought weren't necessarily mad about winning races. The first horse he owned was named Zombie, and it ran true to its name. Bing often averred that his losing stable was purely an altruistic gesture for my benefit, a charitable source of jokes. "Hope is always short of good material," he said.

Bing's penchant for horses eventually got us together in the movies. Wanting to be sure he had good seats at the finish line, Crosby had in his grandly casual way purchased a big interest in the Del Mar racetrack, near San Diego. To boost attendance, he helped stage lavish parties at the track's Turf Club and invited film and radio personalities to entertain. I was included in one of these Saturday-night forays, and Crosby and I did a little reprise of our clowning from the Capitol Theater days. The old chemistry was still there. Only this time a Paramount producer was in the audience, and he said, "We've got to get these two boys together in a picture."

The result was a zany film called *The Road to Singapore* — the first of seven "roads" we traveled on film, usually in pursuit of the lovely Dorothy Lamour. It was Bing who saw the possibilities for ad libbing in the script. I can still see Cros drawing thoughtfully on his pipe between takes as he studied new ways to butcher the script. Sometimes we'd shout back and forth between our dressing rooms, trying out new bits. Poor Dottie Lamour, who had studied her lines like the pro she was, couldn't recognize a single phrase to cue on.

Crosby always loved words, liked to trip them mellifluously over his tongue. He had a soft-spoken way of circumlocution larded with erudite words and foreign phrases that was part of his trademark. (Crosby would have loved those last two sentences.) I remember a scene in *The Road to Morocco* in which we were having trouble with a French policeman. I began ad libbing and asked Cros, "Can you talk French?" "Certainly I can," he replied and directed an effortless stream of Gallic at the policeman. Later I discovered he had recited a short French fable about a crow and a piece of cheese—a classic piece of high-school French that was indelibly imprinted in Bing's brain.

It's no big secret how long I panted after that Barbie-doll-sized gold statue they call Oscar. In fact, it was a running gag between Bing and me, especially after he won one as best actor for his portrayal of Father O'Malley in *Going My Way*. Once, during the filming of *The Road to Rio*, the script had me down on my knees clutching at Crosby's coattails, crying, "Don't leave me! Don't leave me!" As the take drew to a close, Crosby solemnly pulled his Oscar from beneath his coat and handed it to me. The sound stage broke up.

If you want biographical detail on Harry Lillis Crosby, there are several books around (including Bing's own, *Call Me Lucky*) that trace his career from the early days in Spokane to his place in the pantheon of popular entertainers. You can read all about Crosby playing drums with an outfit called the Musicaladers, about his big break with the Paul Whiteman band and the forming of a trio called the "Rhythm Boys." Then, at the fabled Coconut Grove in Los Angeles, Bing began singing solo, and the music business was never quite the same.

The mischievous kid from the big Irish family who had wanted to be a professional baseball player became a recording star before there were recording stars. It's estimated that he sold more than 400 million records and recorded more than 4,000 songs. Then there were the movies and the radio, television and concert appearances.

But nobody has to remind us how big Bing was. I just like to recall the *way* he was.

For all his celluloid escapades, for all his celebrity, Bing was a private man, and he let it be known quite firmly that he intended to live "*outside* the fan magazines." He had the magnificent opportunity to love and be loved by two extraordinary women: his first wife and mother of his four eldest sons, Dixie Lee, who died of cancer in 1952; and Kathryn, the beautiful and vivacious lady who was his wife the last 20 years of his life, bearing him two sons and a daughter.

The public loved him because they saw in him an absolutely ordinary guy who had become very rich and very famous—yet never left his real self behind. Who but Bing could be refused a room at a posh hotel when he came in from a hunting trip all bearded and bedraggled? And it was just like him, too, to be arrested by the Paris police who found him dozing next to a "Keep Off the Grass" sign, a newspaper tented over his face to shut out the sun. He loved singing and show business, but he always let it be known that he might just rather be playing golf, fishing a good trout stream or hunting pheasant with a Labrador at his side.

Make no mistake, though, Bing was serious about those things he believed important in life: family, church and giving his time, talent and money to a world he felt had been pretty good to him. He was a devout Catholic, but he didn't wear his religion on his sleeve. When director Leo McCarey approached him about playing the part of the young priest in *Going My Way*, Bing was concerned that the Church might find the idea of a "crooner" in the role offensive. Only after McCarey assured him that a number of priests had reacted favorably did Bing agree. The result was the portrayal of Father O'Malley that further endeared him to millions.

Bing also had to be practically coerced into recording "Silent Night" and "White Christmas." When Decca asked him to do "Silent Night," he refused, saying it would be like "cashing in" on religion. He relented when it was arranged that the proceeds would go to orphans being taken care of by American missions in China. Later, during the Second World War, Bing and his troupe toured military camps on funds from "Silent Night." It was his next-biggest-selling record to "White Christmas."

"White Christmas," sung by Bing. What more can you say? Who isn't touched with a wave of nostalgia? But again, everyone had to twist Bing's arm to get him to sing it in *Holiday Inn*. He said it might be interpreted as commercializing Christmas. He was finally persuaded, and he sang it like nobody ever will again. It became one of the biggest hits of all time, a special tribute to the man who loved to take his kids caroling in the neighborhood every Christmas.

I don't suppose anyone will ever be able to calculate the total amount of money Crosby gave or raised for charitable causes. He loved golf, particularly when he was playing to raise money for a hospital, school or some other worthy cause. And he sacrificed time, money and even physical stamina to do charity benefits—so much that someone called him a one-man "itinerant foundation."

> # He took potshots at my nose. I fired back at "Ol' Dad" about his thinning hair.

Once we played a charity golf match together in Indianapolis during World War II. I was scheduled to go from there to South Bend for a War Bond rally at Notre Dame. I asked Bing to come along, and he did. The crowd roared with delight at his unexpected entrance. Then he flew on to Chicago, while I stayed in South Bend to do a show at a Navy installation the next day. It was my birthday, and darned if Cros didn't fly back to surprise me onstage with a cake.

He liked those casual surprises. I was in London once doing a benefit for a boys' club and asked Bing, who was also in town, to appear. It was unlikely he could make it, and I didn't really promise that he'd show, but the word got around. That night the audience called to me, "Where's Bing?" I joked with them, saying it was late for such an old man to be out. Suddenly there he was, leaning against the proscenium grinning at me between puffs on his pipe. The crowd went nuts. It was the first time Bing had ever been on the stage in England. He sang for 40 minutes as the audience shouted out their favorites.

In December 1976, Bing and his family began a charity concert tour that showed the world he could still sing like nobody else. Clive Barnes wrote in the New York *Times*, "He lives his songs. He never plays any role other than himself. This is what is so touching."

That was Bing all the way. A natural. One of his old buddies from Spokane said that when Bing was a boy, you could always tell he was coming because you'd hear him singing or whistling. Well, thanks to records and films, he'll never leave us. That's a reassuring and pleasant thought.

Bing loved his dad and said of him, "He was a cheery man. He liked everybody, and I think everybody liked him, which is a better epitaph than most men have."

It's Bing's epitaph, too. If friends could be made to order, I would have asked for one like him. ∎

# Johnson's LIST

Johnnie kept a secret record as his fellow soldiers met their deaths at the hands of a brutal North Korean major. He risked execution, but thought only of the victims' families.

*By Malcolm McConnell*

The sign on the banquet-room door read "Tiger Survivors." The 30 men who gathered that July evening in Evansville, Ind., could have been retirees, perhaps a bowling club. But the tales being told transported them back four decades to freezing mud, starvation, the sickening smack of rifles.

They had been American prisoners of war who lived through three years of captivity, some of it under a brutal North Korean army major the prisoners called The Tiger. In October 1950, he took command of 758 sick and dejected POWs. When repatriation came in August 1953, only 262 were still alive.

At one table the men recalled The Tiger's infamous death march along the Yalu River. They struggled to remember just when one buddy had died.

A quiet man with a careworn face named Wayne "Johnnie" Johnson, 57, rose from his chair. "I'll tell you *exactly* when," he announced.

The others exchanged quizzical glances as Johnson, a newcomer to their reunions, produced a smudgy photocopy protected by clear plastic. Both sides of two and a half pages of narrow notepad paper were crammed with columns of tiny, neatly printed block letters and numbers.

ILLUSTRATION BY OWEN SMITH

"This is my list," Johnnie explained. He scanned the rows, then said that the man had died in a freezing cornfield pen outside of Manp'o, North Korea, before the death march.

Larry Zellers, 66, a Methodist missionary prisoner in the Tiger group, was intrigued. "Where on earth did you get this list, Johnnie?"

"Well," Johnson replied with a soft Southwestern twang, "it's a long story. ..."

**PFC Johnnie Johnson, from Lima, Ohio,** was just 18 when his division, the 24th Infantry, was thrown into combat in the summer of 1950. Their mission: a desperate attempt to slow the massive communist invasion of South Korea.

On July 11, 1950, less than three weeks into the war, Johnson was captured. A few nights later American planes accidentally strafed a building where he and other POWs were being held. Several men were killed. *Somebody might forget these guys,* Johnnie thought. *But their families have the right to know where and when they died.* Using a pencil stub, he carefully wrote down on a scrap of paper their names, units and dates of death.

By late October the North Koreans were pushed north by American-led allied forces. Huddled in a pen in the village of Manp'o and fed wormy, half cooked millet, most of Johnson's POW group were sick and malnourished. Seventy were already dead, including seven executed. Johnson listed each name on scraps torn from guards' discarded cigarette packages and a strip of wallpaper he'd ripped from a schoolhouse. *We'll be home soon,* Johnnie hoped, *and the families will know the truth.*

Then The Tiger took command. "We are going on a long march," he announced. A priest protested that the POWs were too weak. "Then let them march until they die," The Tiger replied.

For nine days the POWs marched across 120 miles of steep mountain terrain. Despite bitterly cold November weather, the prisoners wore only summer fatigues. The guards promised that the sick who fell out would be picked up by ox carts. But as the POWs climbed the next ridge, they heard gunshots.

The Tiger threatened to execute American officers for failing to keep the column moving quickly. They protested. He exploded in a rage. "Then I will shoot only the officer whose group lost the most men." Army 1st Lt. Cordus H. Thornton stepped forward. The Tiger put his pistol to Thornton's head and fired.

Then he ordered the stunned POWs to turn in their dog tags. "Forget dead men," he shouted. Risking execution if he was caught, Johnson managed to jot down the names of over a hundred men who died in the snowy mountains.

That winter, in the prison camp on the ice-choked Yalu River, was one of the coldest in Korean history. Almost 300 more prisoners died, many in unheated huts where guards abandoned the sick. Johnson added their names to his secret list, now kept on dozens of scraps of paper stuffed into a small cloth pouch.

In October 1951, the surviving prisoners were transferred to Chinese control. After hearing rumors of a prisoner exchange, Johnson began compiling a master list on paper he'd stolen from a guard's notepad. Working each night for months by the light of a crude oil lamp, he made two identical lists and hid one in the mud-hut wall, the other in the dirt floor.

One sleety morning Chinese guards discovered the list after digging out the patch of wall where it was hidden. "You keep this criminal propaganda for your government," charged the Chinese major.

"It's not propaganda, sir," Johnson replied, trying to subdue his fear. "It's for the families."

The commandant began to beat Johnnie's face with a thick leather riding crop. "Who helped you?"

"I'm acting on my own."

For an hour the commandant methodically whipped Johnson, repeating the questions. But Johnson didn't break. Finally the commandant thrust the muzzle of a .45-caliber pistol against Johnson's head. "Eventually you will tell me the truth," he said, cocking the gun. Inexplicably, he didn't fire.

When he returned to his hut, Johnnie knew that he should destroy the second list. Then he pictured his closest friend, Raymond Alford, who died of beriberi at a camp in An-dong and was buried without dog tags in an unmarked grave. No, his list must reach the hundreds of families like Alford's. It remained hidden in the floor.

In August 1953, the 262 Tiger survivors were ordered to prepare for repatriation. Johnnie dug up his list. At the processing camp the POWs received Red Cross relief packages that included toothpaste. Peeling open the tube, he cleaned out the interior as best he could and sealed the list inside.

Not until he was safely on a troopship home did he bring the list out. Intelligence officers asked the POWs to write the names of buddies who had died in captivity. Johnnie sat at a table, his precious list spread before him. An officer approached: "What have you got there?"

"It's my list, sir," Johnnie explained. "I kept it for the families." The officer held up the thin sheets of notepaper crammed with the tight columns of names. Quietly Johnson added, "There's 496 on the list."

A lieutenant made a brief note in Johnnie's debriefing report: "Subject very cooperative—has recorded names, dates & places—should be commended." But as America tried to forget the tragedy of Korea, the record of Johnson's list slipped into bureaucratic oblivion.

**Freedom did not bring peace** to Johnnie Johnson. Haunted by nightmares, he sought solace in alcohol. He moved from one job to another, and four marriages ended in divorce. Not until the 1980s, when he was treated for post-traumatic stress disorder, was he able to resume a normal life. In all that time, the military never sought out his list.

The men at the reunion listened, shaken. "Your list is important, Johnnie," said Wilbert "Shorty" Estabrook, one of his buddies from the camp and founder of the Tiger Survivors. He had tried for years to reconstruct an accurate roster of dead Tiger group members. "Can you work with us?" he asked.

"I'd be proud to," Johnson replied.

But residual toothpaste had faded the ink on several columns, blotting out almost a quarter of the names. The men asked for help from forensic document examiner Howard Birnbaum at the Arizona Department of Public Safety in Phoenix, where Johnnie lived.

Birnbaum gently placed the 40-year-old list in an infrared scanning device, and phantom images began to emerge. "Roger ... Hart ... man," Johnnie read. It was 1st Lt. Roger W. Hartman, an artillery officer who had died at the An-dong camp in February 1951.

Working tirelessly, Johnson and Birnbaum were able to reconstruct more than 100 of the previously illegible entries. By the summer of 1991 the restored list contained most of the 496 names Johnnie had compiled.

Johnnie, Estabrook and retired Army Command Sgt. Maj. Tim Casey compared the names against the official records. They were astounded to learn that most of the men were still officially classified as missing in action. What's more, in 1953 the communists had given the U.N. Command the names of 147 POWs who they claimed escaped from captivity. In fact, Johnnie's list showed that most had been executed. Still, they couldn't contact the next of kin because the Privacy Act prevented the Pentagon from releasing their addresses.

**Mary Lou Hoolihan, 47, of St. Cloud, Minn.,** flew to Denver the summer of 1991, torn by optimism and anxiety. Her father, 1st Lt. George Kristanoff, had disappeared while leading a reconnaissance patrol in July 1950. As a child, she had spent hours studying fading press clippings about her dad.

The Army sent a presumptive finding of death in 1954, but uncertainty remained. The communists claimed that Kristanoff was one of the 147 American POWs who had escaped. Mary Lou's family believed he may have been recaptured and was being held hostage. Decades passed, but the aching wound of her father's fate was unhealed. Then, by chance, she heard of the 1991 Tiger Survivors reunion in Denver.

Johnnie listened intently to Mary Lou's story. He then sorted through his papers and handed her a photocopy of his list. "His name is here," he said tenderly, his finger gliding to the upper right-hand column: *George Kristanoff 1L, 24 Rec, 4-29-51.*

First Lt. George Kristanoff of the 24th Reconnaissance Company had died in An-dong prison camp on April 29, 1951. Mary Lou's eyes filled with tears. Then she felt a release she had never before experienced. "I *had* to find out what really happened to my father," she told Johnnie, her voice growing strong.

Now Johnnie's deeply lined face was wet with tears. He took Mary Lou's hand. "After 40 years I've been able to help one family," he said, his voice breaking. "Risking my life was worthwhile."

Johnson, Estabrook and Casey were able to help a dozen other families as well. At a 1993 Tiger Survivors reunion, retired teacher Gerald Doyle, 68, gave an anguished account of his youngest brother, Austin. A Navy reservist in 1949, Gerald had persuaded their mother to allow Austin to enlist "so he'd have a chance to grow up." When Austin's unit was thrown into combat, Gerald asked to be activated and sent to Korea. He was processing for overseas when the family received news that Austin was missing. "If I hadn't asked Mom to let him enlist, he'd still be alive," Gerald said.

In 1953, the Army wrote that Austin had died in 1951 but that the information was unverified. "Even after all these years," Gerald Doyle said, "I need to know how he really died."

Estabrook handed Doyle a roster. "You can trust this list," he explained.

Doyle read the words he had both dreaded and longed to find. PFC Lawrence Austin Doyle had died in the pen at Manp'o on October 28, 1950, just before the death march began.

The survivors explained that Austin had been among the sick separated from the group. Most of these young soldiers understood they would be executed after the column left. They readily gave their boots to the comrades who needed them. "I've never seen braver men," a survivor told Doyle.

**Army Reserve Sgt. Victoria Bingham** of the Defense Department's POW/MIA Office attended the Korean War Ex-POW Association's reunion in Sacramento, Calif., in 1995. She was electrified by accounts of Johnson's heroic action and touched by the comfort his list was bringing. She embarked on a crusade to have Johnson decorated for valor.

A search of intelligence archives yielded Johnson's original debriefing report and other POW reports that corroborated his story. At long last the names are being incorporated into the POW/MIA Office's database. Analysts confirm that the list is incredibly accurate.

On August 3, 1996, America finally thanked Johnnie Johnson for his "exemplary courage and selfless determination to provide a record of deceased soldiers, even in the face of death by a hostile enemy." Pinning the Silver Star, the nation's third-highest medal for valor, on Johnson's chest, Lt. Gen. John E. Miller said, "I'm very glad to see you receive this award, even though it has taken a very long time for you to be recognized."

Johnnie Johnson's comrades-in-arms exploded in applause. ∎

# LOU Gehrig's

## By Paul Gallico

Known as the Iron Horse because he never missed a game, he became an even greater legend with this farewell speech.

I remember writing years ago: "There is no greater inspiration to any American boy than Lou Gehrig. For if the awkward, inept and downright clumsy player that I knew in the beginning could through sheer drive and determination turn himself into the finest first-base-covering machine in all baseball, then nothing is impossible to any man or boy in this country."

# EPIC *of* COURAGE

The last chapter in the life of this baseball hero puts a big exclamation point after that statement. Gehrig was at the height of his career. From the press box, sports writers looked down with honest affection at the piano legs, the broad rear porch that had earned him the name of Biscuit Pants, the powerful shoulders and the pleasant face of "that big dumb Dutchman."

From 1936 through 1938, with Gehrig as captain, the Yankees won three World Series in a row. In 1936, Lou was for the second time named the most valuable player in the American League, nine years after he had first

# Lou played with fevers, fractures and a concussion that would have put someone else in the hospital for weeks.

achieved this honor. And his consecutive-game record went on and on. Sick or well, he never missed a game. Lou played in spite of colds, in spite of fevers. He played so doubled over with lumbago that he couldn't straighten up—and, though bent over at the plate, he still got himself a single.

One year he fractured a toe. He played on. Knocked unconscious by a wild pitch and suffering from a concussion that would hospitalize the average man for two weeks, he was at his position the next day *and collected four hits.* When, late in his career, his hands were X-rayed, they found 17 assorted fractures that had healed by themselves. He had broken every finger on both hands, and some twice, and hadn't even mentioned it to anyone.

The fantastic thing about all this is not that Lou was able to endure the pain of breaks, sprains and torn tendons, but that it failed to impair his efficiency. If he had something the matter with him, he tried all the harder.

The slow tragedy of disintegration began in the winter of 1938–39 when Lou, a fine skater, fell repeatedly on the ice. The following spring, finding himself slow in training, he began to drive his body harder to make up for its mysterious failure. When the symptoms of his slowing up were obvious at St. Petersburg training quarters, the sports writers sadly wrote that the old Iron Horse was

running down. But the players on the Yankee ball club knew that a ballplayer slows up gradually—he doesn't come apart all at once.

There are grim tales of things that happened in the locker room. One tells of Gehrig leaning over to lace his shoes and falling forward to the floor, to lie helpless; and of tough men with fine instinct to look away and not to hurt him by offering help as he struggled to his feet.

Among elements that go to make up a hero is the capacity for quiet, uncomplaining suffering. This was Lou Gehrig. Not even his wife Eleanor knew how terribly he suffered during those days when his speed and skill were deserting him, when he found, to his bewilderment, that he could not bat, could not run, could not field. The nightmare strain and terror of it lined his face in a few short months and brought gray to his hair. But it could not force a complaint from his lips.

When it became apparent that there was something wrong, Lou drove himself still more relentlessly. It never occurred to him to blame something beyond his control. His performance during the early part of 1939 was pitiful. And yet, so great was the spell cast by his honest attempts to please and his service over the long years that the worst-mannered individual in the world, the baseball fan, forbore to heckle him.

On Sunday, April 30, 1939, the Yankees played the Senators. At first, Lou muffed an easy throw; he came to bat four times with runners on base, failed even to meet the ball, and the Yankees lost.

Monday was an off day. Gehrig did a lot of thinking. He had the toughest decision of his life to make. Tuesday the team played the Tigers. Lou went to Manager McCarthy in the dugout. "Joe," he said slowly, "I always said that when I felt I couldn't help the team any more I would take myself out of the line-up. I guess that time has come."

"When do you want to quit, Lou?" asked McCarthy.

Gehrig looked at him steadily and said, "Now."

His consecutive-games record ended at 2,130 games.

Lou went to the Mayo Clinic for a checkup. The Yankees released the doctors' diagnosis: It was a form of paralysis. The cause of the sudden, mysterious decline of Henry Louis Gehrig was solved.

Before Gehrig came home from the Mayo, his wife went to their family physician, told him the name of the disease and asked the truth. He told her that her husband could not live more than two years. Eleanor telephoned the Clinic. She learned that the doctors had not had the heart to tell Lou. "Please promise me that you never will let him know," she begged.

Lou came home full of smiles and jokes, and the girl who met him was gay, too, though neither noticed that in the laughter of the other there was something feverish. They were too busy with their magnificent deception of each other. Eleanor fought a constant fight to keep the truth from Lou. As to what Lou knew, he never told anybody.

On July 4, 1939, there took place the most tragic scene ever enacted on a baseball diamond—the funeral services for Henry Louis Gehrig.

Lou attended them in person.

Lou Gehrig Appreciation Day, it was called, a gesture of love and appreciation, a spontaneous reaching out to a man who had been good and kind and decent, to thank him for having been so.

The most touching demonstration was the coming from the ends of the country of Gehrig's former teammates, the famous Yankees of 1927.

And there was George Herman Ruth. The Babe and Lou hadn't got along very well in the last years they played together. But despite their childish feud, the Babe was here now with an arm around Lou and a whispered pleasantry that came at a time when Gehrig was very near collapse from emotions that turmoiled within him.

The principal speakers were Postmaster General Jim Farley and Mayor La Guardia; 61,808 were in the stands. It was what was known as a Great Day.

To Lou Gehrig it was goodbye to everyone that he had known and loved.

In a box in the stands were those he held dear: his mother and father, unaware of his doom, and his wife. Lifelong friends were there, and as Lou observed them gathered in his honor, he knew he was seeing them thus for the last time.

Gifts piled up for him: a silver service, smoking sets, writing sets, fishing tackle. They were from the Yankees; from their great rivals, the Giants; from the baseball writers; even from the ushers and peanut boys in the stadium. The warmth of the feeling that prompted their presentation melted the iron reserve in Lou and broke him down.

It was so human and so heroic that Gehrig should have wept there in public—not for the pity of himself, nor for the beauty and sweetness of the world he would soon leave, but because the boy who all his life had convinced himself that he had no worth now understood for the first time how much people loved him.

Not only were his immediate family, his adored wife and his personal friends broadcasting their warmth to him but a great throng of plain, simple people with whom he felt a deep kinship. To tune in suddenly upon so much love was nearly too much for him.

The speeches were ended at last, and the stadium rocked with wave after wave of cheers. Lou stood with head bowed to the tumult and pressed a handkerchief to his eyes.

When at last he faced the microphones, the noise stopped abruptly. Everyone waited for what he would say. With a finger he dashed away the tears that would not stay back, lifted his head and spoke his epitaph:

"For the past two weeks you have been reading about a bad break I got. Yet today I consider myself the luckiest man on the face of the earth. ..."

Although the tale of Lou Gehrig really ends above, perhaps in the simple story of how he lived what time was left to him is to be found his greatest gallantry. Those two years called for the most difficult heroism of all—the heroism of the laugh that covers pain and the light phrase that denies hopelessness and a sinking heart.

Lou chose to spend his last days not in one final feverish attempt to suck from life in two years all that he might have had in 40 but in work and service.

Mayor La Guardia appointed him a city parole commissioner. And so for the next months, as long as he was able

> "For the past two weeks you have been reading about a bad break I got. Yet today I consider myself the luckiest man on the face of the earth."

to walk, even with the assistance of others, Gehrig went daily to his office. He listened to the cases, studied them; he brought to the job his thoroughness and his innate kindness and understanding.

He sat at his desk even when no longer able to move his arms. When he wanted a cigarette, his wife or secretary lit it for him, put it between his lips and removed it to shake the ash.

He listened to thief, vagabond, narcotic addict and prostitute. When there was help to be given, he gave it unstintingly from what strength there was left to him. He would not give in. He did not give in.

On June 2, 1941, Lou Gehrig died in the arms of his wife in their home in Riverdale, N.Y. ∎

By A. J. Cronin

# The Best Investment I Ever Made

**The stranger wanted to tell him a secret. It wasn't what he expected.**

ILLUSTRATION BY JEAN-MARIE BENOIT

On the second day out from New York, while making the round of the promenade deck, I suddenly became aware that one of the other passengers was watching me closely, following me with his gaze every time I passed, his eyes filled with a queer, almost pathetic intensity.

I have crossed the Atlantic many times. And on this occasion, tired after a prolonged piece of work, I wanted to rest, to avoid the tedium of casual and importunate shipboard contacts. I gave no sign of having noticed the man.

Yet there was nothing importunate about him. On the contrary, he seemed affected by a troubled, rather touching diffidence. He was in his early 40s, I judged—out of the corner of my eye—rather short in build, with a fair complexion, a good forehead from which his thin hair had begun to recede and clear blue eyes. His dark suit, sober tie and rimless spectacles gave evidence of a serious and reserved disposition.

At this point the bugle sounded for dinner, and I went below. On the following forenoon, I again observed my fellow voyager watching me earnestly from his deck chair.

Now a lady was with him, obviously his wife. She was about his age, quiet and restrained, with brown eyes and slightly faded brown hair, dressed in a gray skirt and gray woolen cardigan.

The situation by this time had begun to intrigue me, and from my steward I discovered that they were Mr. and Mrs. John S———, from a small suburb of London. Yet when another day passed without event, I began to feel certain that Mr. S——— would remain too shy to carry out his obvious desire to approach me. However, on our final evening at sea Mrs. S——— decided the matter. With a firm pressure on his hand and a whispered word in his ear, she urged her husband toward me as I passed along the deck.

"Excuse me, Doctor. I wonder if I might introduce myself." He spoke almost breathlessly, offering me the visiting card he held in his hand and studying my face to see if the name meant anything to me. Then, as it plainly did not, he went on with the same awkwardness. "If you could spare a few minutes ... my wife and I would so like to have a word with you."

A moment later I was occupying the vacant chair beside them. Haltingly he told me that this had been their first visit to America. It was not entirely a holiday trip. They had been making a tour of the New England states, inspecting many of the summer recreational camps provided for young people there. Afterward, they had visited settlement houses in New York and other cities to study the methods employed in dealing with youth groups, especially backward, maladjusted and delinquent cases.

There was in his voice and manner, indeed in his whole personality, a genuine enthusiasm that was disarming. I found myself liking him instinctively. Questioning him further, I learned that he and his wife had been active for the past 15 years in the field of youth welfare. He was, by profession, a solicitor, but in addition to his practice at the courts, found time to act as director of a charitable organization devoted to the care of boys and girls, mostly from city slums, who had fallen under the ban of the law.

As he spoke with real feeling, I got a vivid picture of the work these two people were doing—how they took derelict adolescents from the juvenile courts and, placing them in a healthy environment, healed them in mind and body, sent them back into the world, trained in a useful handicraft and fit to take their place as worthy members of the community.

It was a work of redemption that stirred the heart, and I asked what had directed his life into this channel. The question had a strange effect upon him; he took a sharp breath and exclaimed,

"You still do not remember me?"

I shook my head: To the best of my belief I had never in my life seen him before.

"I've wanted to get in touch with you for many years," he went on, under increasing stress. "But I was never able to bring myself to do so." Then, bending near, he spoke a few words, tensely, in my ear. At that, slowly, the veils parted,

"Excuse me, Doctor. I wonder if I might introduce myself. If you could spare a few minutes, my wife and I would so like to have a word with you."

my thoughts sped back a quarter of a century, and with a start, I remembered the sole occasion when I had seen this man before.

I was a young doctor at the time and had just set up in practice in a working-class district of London. On a foggy November night, toward one o'clock, I was awakened by a loud banging on the door. In those days of economic necessity any call, even at this unearthly hour, was a welcome one. Hurriedly, I threw on some clothes and went downstairs. It was a sergeant of police, in dripping helmet and cape, mistily outlined on the doorstep. A suicide case, he told me abruptly, in the lodgings around the corner—I had better come at once.

Outside it was raw and damp, the traffic stilled, the street deserted, quiet as the tomb. We walked the short distance in silence, even our footsteps muffled by the fog, and turned into the narrow entrance of an old building.

As we mounted the creaking staircase, my nostrils were stung by the sick-sweet odor of illuminating gas. On the upper story the agitated landlady showed us to a bare little attic where, stretched on a narrow bed, lay the body of a young man.

Although apparently lifeless, there remained the barest chance that the youth was not quite beyond recall. With the sergeant's help, I began the work of resuscitation. For an entire hour we labored without success. A further 15 minutes, and despite our most strenuous exertions, it appeared useless. Then, as we were about to give up, completely exhausted, there broke from the patient a shallow, convulsive gasp. It was like a resurrection from the grave, a miracle, this stirring of life under our hands. Half an hour of redoubled efforts and we had the youth sitting up, gazing at us dazedly and, alas, slowly realizing the horror of his situation.

He was a round-cheeked lad, with a simple, countrified air, and the story that he told us as he slowly regained strength in the bleak morning hours was simple, too. His parents were dead. An uncle in the provinces, anxious, no doubt, to be rid of an unwanted responsibility, had found him a position as clerk in a London solicitor's office. He had been in the city only six months. Utterly friendless, he had fallen victim to the loose society of the streets, had made bad companions and, like a young fool, eager to taste pleasure far beyond his means, had begun to bet on horses. Soon he had lost all his small savings, had pledged his belongings and owed the bookmaker a disastrous amount. In an effort to recoup, he had taken a sum of money from the office safe for a final gamble that, he was assured, was certain to win. But this last resort had failed. Terrified of the prosecution that must follow, sick at heart,

sunk in despair, he had shut himself in his room and turned on the gas.

A long bar of silence throbbed in the little attic when he concluded this halting confession. Then, gruffly, the sergeant asked how much he had stolen. Pitifully, almost, the answer came: seven pounds ten shillings. Yes, incredible though it seemed, for this paltry sum this poor misguided lad had almost thrown away his life.

Again there came a pause in which, plainly, the same unspoken thought was uppermost in the minds of the three of us who were the sole witnesses of this near tragedy. Almost of one accord, we voiced our desire to give the youth—whose defenseless nature rather than any vicious tendencies had brought him to this extremity—a fresh start.

> Slowly, the doctor's thoughts sped back a full quarter of a century. With a start, he remembered the only time he had seen this fellow before.

The sergeant, at considerable risk to his job, resolved to make no report upon the case, so that no court proceedings would result. The landlady offered a month's free board until he should get upon his feet again. While I, making perhaps the least contribution, came forward with seven pounds ten shillings for him to put back in the office safe.

**The ship moved on through the still darkness** of the night. There was no need of speech. With a tender gesture Mrs. S——— had taken her husband's hand. And as we sat in silence, hearing the sounding of the sea and the sighing of the breeze, a singular emotion overcame me. I could not but reflect that, against all the bad investments I had made throughout the years—those foolish speculations for material gain, producing only anxiety, disappointment and frustration—here at last was one I need not regret, one that had paid no dividends in worldly goods, yet which might stand, nevertheless on the profit side, in the final reckoning. ∎

# Diana & the Queen

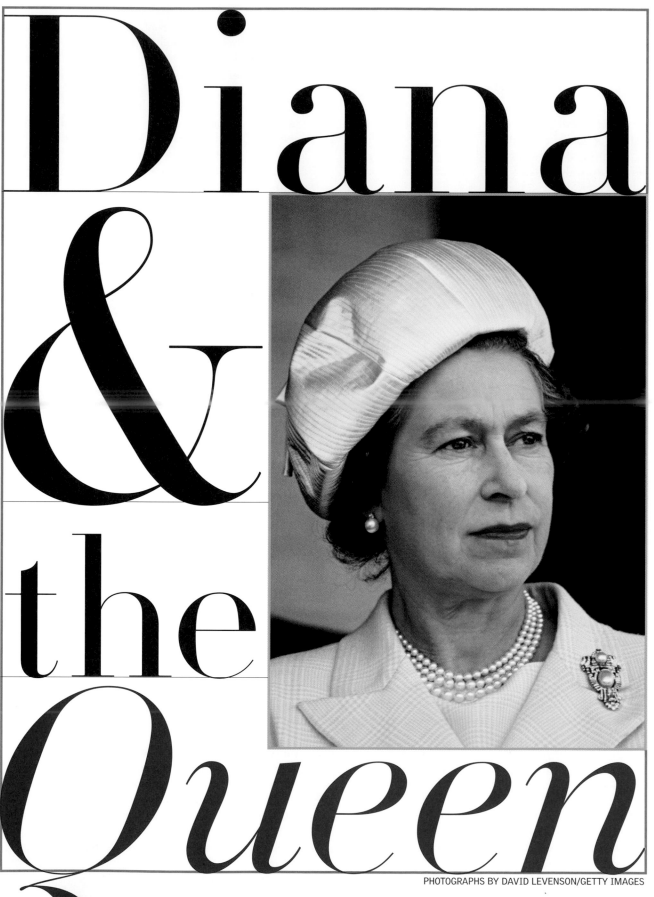

*By*
*Ingrid Seward*

They knew they needed each other. But Elizabeth, proper in her hats and pearls, was driven by a rigid sense of protocol. And she grew weary and wary of the insecure, indiscreet, unpredictable Princess Di.

The tragic news that Diana, Princess of Wales, had died in a Paris car crash came to us in August, four years ago. As Americans watched her funeral pageant at Westminster Abbey, it was easy to think of her only as a princess, someone completely unlike the rest of us.

But within the royal family Diana was an all-too-human relative. She doted on her sons, William and Harry. She loved and fought with Prince Charles, her estranged husband. And she had a complicated relationship with the Queen, her mother-in-law, alternately viewing her as a substitute mom and a meddling old woman who was out to get her.

In *The Queen and Di*, British author Ingrid Seward, who has covered the royal family for 18 years, draws on knowledge from her own sources to show

PHOTOGRAPHS BY DAVID LEVENSON/GETTY IMAGES

how Diana and the Queen were close to being each other's salvation. When the Princess held a sick orphan or wore a stunning gown, she warmed the otherwise cold and at times even weird public image of the royal family. The Queen, meanwhile, offered Diana a chance to find the home life she had been missing—Diana's own mother had left home, and a broken marriage, when Diana was only six. But the Princess's psychological problems, and the Queen's rigid sense of protocol and propriety, ultimately undermined their relationship.

In her new book, Seward recounts the morning of August 31, when the Queen and Prince Charles heard about Diana's accident. The Princess and her lover, Dodi Fayed, were trying to escape a crowd of paparazzi when their driver lost control in an underpass. Almost immediately, the news flashed to Balmoral, the Queen's country home in Scotland.

**The Queen was awakened** in the early hours of the morning. Pulling on her old-fashioned dressing gown, she went into the corridor where she met Prince Charles. The news from Paris was that Dodi Fayed was dead, but Diana had survived. Soon the whole castle stirred from its slumber. Charles took incoming calls. The Queen ordered tea, which was brought from the kitchen and then ignored.

Their first concern was to discover how badly injured Diana was. Initially they were told that she had walked away from the accident virtually unscathed. Then another call came through. "Sir, I am very sorry to have to tell you that I've just had the Ambassador on the phone. The Princess died a short time ago."

Charles's composure collapsed, and the tears the public never saw began to flow. The Queen was equally stunned. While others in the royal family had long since given up on Diana, Elizabeth had retained some affection for her daughter-in-law and still sympathized with her. She recognized Diana's potential—and saw her death as a terrible waste.

In the outpouring of grief from Diana's supporters, the royal family found itself caught in a startling rip of public rancor. Crowds surged through the streets of London mourning the Princess, and the Palace was blamed for treating her heartlessly. Perhaps for the first time in her life Queen Elizabeth had to ask: What do they want me to do?

**I once asked Diana whether her marriage had been arranged,** and she told me with some irritation, "It was Charles and I who decided on the marriage. Not the Queen. Us. No one else."

That was true—no one ordered Charles to propose or Diana to accept. Without the Queen's approval, though, no proposal would have been made.

As their romance acquired momentum, almost everyone urged Charles to press forward. The Queen herself never directly addressed the question of marriage, but by nod and nuance she made it clear she approved of Diana. The Prince, however, was confused. "I'm terrified sometimes of making a promise and then perhaps living to regret it," he said.

The question, when it came, was a question in itself. "If I were to ask, what do you think you might say?" Charles inquired. Giggling, Diana replied, "Yeah, okay." Charles then ran out of the room to telephone his mother with the news.

The engagement was announced on February 24, 1981, and Diana soon moved into rooms at Buckingham Palace. Since Diana had been born into privilege, the Queen believed her future daughter-in-law knew what was expected of her. As she wrote to a friend in March 1981, "I trust that Diana will find living here less of a burden than is expected."

**In fact Diana had no notion of what to expect**—and from the beginning she found royal life an extraordinary burden. She swam most mornings in the Palace pool, immersed herself in wedding plans and took dance and exercise classes. The rest of the time she simply sat around, bored and increasingly irritable.

Pent-up and lonely, Diana began making herself ill, the first signs of bulimia. Several times a day she visited the kitchen, filling a bowl with Kellogg's Frosted Flakes and fruit, adding sugar and drenching it all in cream. Afterward she would go to the bathroom and make herself sick.

Her moods became ever more unpredictable, and Charles drew much of her fire. Why, she asked, was he not spending more time with her? It was explained that the Prince had a schedule of engagements arranged months before. That did little to pacify her.

The Queen chose to overlook Diana's behavior in these early months, concluding that she needed time to settle in. Nearly everyone, from the Queen to the staff who looked after Diana, attributed her behavior to a bad case of "nerves."

Left to struggle through, Diana did so, barely. After one particularly difficult stretch in June 1981, when the Prince was traveling, she bolted. Following a party to celebrate Prince Andrew's twenty-first birthday, she got into her car at 5:30 a.m. and drove from London to her family home, over an hour away. She told her father, John Spencer, that she was calling off the engagement. He listened as Diana poured out her heart, then advised

her that it was probably just the pressure. Once she was married, said her father, things would get easier.

By Sunday night Diana was back in Buckingham Palace, acting as if nothing had happened.

**Most brides revel in the first few weeks of marriage.** Instead, during her honeymoon cruise in the Mediterranean, Diana became violently ill with bulimia. After 15 exhausting days, which were punctuated by tremendous fights, the newlyweds arrived back at Balmoral. The Prince summoned a doctor, the first of many who would try to help. "All the analysts and psychiatrists you could ever dream of came plodding in to sort me out," Diana recalled.

In medical terms, some feel that Diana suffered from borderline personality disorder. Symptoms include fear of abandonment, a tendency toward histrionic behavior, a need for adoration and mood swings. Bulimia can be another manifestation.

The Queen was understanding of Diana's difficulties, especially after it was made clear just how unwell her

> # After a party, Diana got into her car at 5:30 a.m. and drove to her family home. She told her father that she was calling off the engagement.

daughter-in-law was. For all her reserve, Elizabeth seemed to have a natural empathy with Diana. And for a time Diana saw the Queen's support as a source of enormous comfort. "I have the best mother-in-law in the world," she once told me.

**But the Queen's indulgence could not bridge the gulf** between Diana and Charles. Diana was an exuberant city girl barely into her 20s, with zero experience in romance. Charles was a contemplative, self-described "countryman," with several significant love affairs behind him.

The Queen hoped that the births of Prince William, in 1982, and Harry, two years later, would ease the tensions and give Charles and Diana reasons to grow together. Instead, the pressures on the couple increased. Diana's emotional difficulties grew worse, and in short order the marriage began to curdle.

As it did, Diana began calling at Buckingham Palace seeking guidance from her mother-in-law. At first, the Queen took a tolerant view of these unscheduled visits. "Diana was usually in a lot better mood when she left than she was when she arrived," one of the Queen's staff recalled.

In time, though, Elizabeth came to dread the meetings. After one session a footman said, "The Princess cried three times in a half an hour while she was waiting to see you." The Queen replied, "I had her for an hour—and she cried nonstop."

Diana went in search of comfort wherever she could find it and, by 1986, had formed a close relationship with Capt. James Hewitt of the Queen's Household Cavalry.

# The Queen had once compared Diana to "a nervy racehorse," who needed careful handling, not harsh discipline. She thought Di would settle down.

Charles also resumed a relationship with Camilla Parker Bowles, a married woman who many believed was the love of his life.

Queen Elizabeth was advised of these unhappy developments. She had once likened Diana to a "nervy racehorse" who needed careful handling, not harsh discipline. Despite the evidence, she convinced herself that if Diana were given the independence she claimed she needed, her self-assurance would grow and she would settle down.

Instead, what came next was the June 1992 publication of Andrew Morton's book *Diana, Her True Story*. The scandalizing bestseller cast Charles in the worst light, and painted a picture of a royal family so cold and self-absorbed that it was incapable of responding to the plight of a young woman who should have been at its very heart.

Although she was not quoted directly, it was clear Diana collaborated on the book. The Queen was stunned. She was well aware how unhappy her daughter-in-law was, but never imagined Diana would air dirty linen in such a way. In most families, this behavior would have meant the immediate end of the marriage. Instead, the Queen ordered a six-month cooling-off period. Charles agreed. So did Diana. For all her grievances, the Princess realized what life would be like if she were cast out of the royal family altogether.

**Through all of this, Diana presented** a captivating image of beauty and compassion. The gossip magazines might print acres of stories about arguments and illicit affairs, but Diana carried on with her appointments, and the public never stopped adoring her. She also had a genuine sympathy for the ill and troubled. In a royal family desperately in need of a human face, she was the only one who could kneel to comfort a sick child and look as if she meant it.

As much as anyone, Elizabeth saw the good that Diana could do for the monarchy. Yet as the Princess increasingly went her own way—for instance, when she gave a TV interview and questioned whether Charles had the moral character to be king—she became more and more of a liability. Charles and Diana had separated late in 1992; they were divorced in August 1996. And barely a year later, she was dead.

In the end, Diana was the one person the Queen never learned to handle. She reacted badly to criticism—any rebuke by the Queen was taken as an instance of the family ganging up on her. Neither patience nor the silent, steely-eyed displeasure Elizabeth had learned to deploy with such withering effect made any impression on Diana. Yet by doing nothing, and by allowing Diana to disregard the constraints of convention that keep the monarchy in place, the Queen unwittingly allowed the Princess to run out of control.

From the perspective of today, marrying into the House of Windsor is certainly no fairytale; Charles, Princess Anne and Prince Andrew have all gone through divorce. Looking back on the litter of her children's broken marriages, the Queen would come to wonder if she had failed in her duty as a mother. Or, as she once asked of a lady-in-waiting, "Where did we go wrong?" ■

# HUMOR **IN UNIFORM**

**STATIONED IN KOREA** with the Army's 2nd Infantry, I was amazed at how each unit twisted the division's unofficial motto of "Fit to Fight." For instance, the aviation battalion changed the motto to "Fit for Flight." The band modified it to "Fit to Delight." My favorite version, however, was the sign at the dentist's office: "Fit to Bite."

-LARRY J. SIMONE

**THE THEATER GROUP** at our Navy base delayed the opening curtain until well after the 8 p.m. starting time because the commanding officer was still conspicuously absent from his reserved front-row seat. Since we were all aware of military protocol, everyone waited patiently. When a member of our drama club finally spotted the captain settling into his seat, we quickly dimmed the lights. That's when we heard the captain proclaim to his wife, "Great luck! We made it just in time."

-LEE R. FEATHERINGHAM

**AS A PROFESSOR** at Southwest Baptist University in Bolivar, Mo., I often begin class by telling a story about my son who attends the U.S. Naval Academy. Last December, one ingenious student left me a note on the blackboard, wishing me a merry Christmas with the following words: "Feliz Navydad!"

-BING B. BAYER

**AFTER COMPLETING** medical officers basic training, I was assigned to a small Army post in a Boston suburb. I arrived after dark and was directed to my quarters.

The next morning a noncommissioned officer escorted me to the commander's office. As we exited the barracks, I looked toward Massachusetts Bay and noticed the back of a large curved device supported by a labyrinth of steel girders.

Anxious to impress the NCO with my new knowledge of the Army's air-defense system, I pointed to the structure and said, "So that's our primary target acquisition radar?"

"No, sir," the sergeant replied. "That's the back of the drive-in movie screen."

-ANGELO J. ITALIANO

**MY UNIT** at Fort Bliss in Texas was detailed with guard duty. However, since live ammunition was reserved for sensitive locations, our rifles were issued with unloaded magazines. One day while we stood at attention for inspection, the officer in charge confronted a private and barked, "What is the maximum effective range of your M-16, soldier?"

The hapless private glanced down at his empty rifle and replied, "As far as I can throw it, sir."

-JAN GETTING

**REPORTING TO** Camp Lejeune, I was glad my husband had already explained to me that a "Commissioned Officers Mess (open)" is open to all officers, whereas a "Commissioned Officers Mess (closed)" is limited to officers residing on base.

Therefore, I understood this message: "During the holidays the Commissioned Officers Mess (open) will be closed. The Commissioned Officers Mess (closed) will be open."

-PATRICIA W. MINER

**MY FORMER** boyfriend, Duncan, was an officer in the Naval Reserve. One day while stopped at a red light, his car was rear-ended. As the other driver, a sailor, approached, his eyes widened when he saw the lieutenant's uniform.

"It gets even better," Duncan said with a smirk. "I'm also a lawyer."

-BATYAH CHLIEK

# Saving Michael Bowen

## The doctors were stumped. So Shelley had to track down a cure for her son by herself.

*By Lynn Rosellini*

The worst thing was not knowing. Shelley Bowen could handle anything, she thought, as she sped along the 15-mile drive to the emergency room in Tampa, Fla. But this enemy killing her two toddler sons, this scourge of diarrhea and infections and heart palpitations that sent her racing to the hospital at all hours of the day and night, this was a horror that had no name.

"I can't do this!" she railed inwardly. "I'm not smart enough. I don't have the education." But self-pity was not an option.

Shelley Bowen's transformation from a hapless mom to an impassioned advocate has all the classic story elements: a ruthless villain, a valiant heroine, child victims and even a white knight. But this is no fairytale.

PHOTOGRAPH BY KELLY LADUKE

Bowen's life seemed close to perfect that day in 1985 when she delivered her first son, a five-pound eight-ounce, blue-eyed bundle she and her husband, Michael, named Evan. But trouble loomed from the start. Evan suffered from hypothermia and jaundice. He didn't gain weight. When the doctors finally let the Bowens take him home after four days, he was so tiny they dressed him in doll clothes.

The baby's first weeks were a nightmare. When Shelley tried to breastfeed, he turned away. His body in spasms, Evan cried all the time.

"Something's really wrong," Shelley said to her husband. But when they took Evan to the doctor, they were told not to worry: "It's just colic."

Evan's unexplained fevers, rashes and nonstop crying continued. Adding to the anxiety, Michael Jr., born 13 months later, developed exactly the same symptoms. Both boys suffered from chronic upper-respiratory ailments and an unusual red rash. They had little appetite, slept a great deal and, when awake, sweated profusely.

The doctors were stumped. It was a virus, they said. No, it was an immune deficiency. The rash? Folliculitis. The sweating? Overactive sweat glands. Or was there something wrong in the Bowens' home? A social worker visited to look for signs of child abuse. The boys were tested for cocaine and morphine, and for AIDS as well.

Then, in a final act of humiliation, three public health officers arrived to search the house for drugs. While Shelley sat furious at the dining room table, they rummaged under the kitchen sink, in the bathroom medicine chest, through hall closets and bedroom drawers. They found nothing. There was never anything to find.

Finally, state environmental protection agents condemned the house, labeling the problem "sick house syndrome" because it had been built over a cow pasture pond.

Shelley Bowen, a high school dropout who worked as a dental assistant, had been raised to think that the word of doctors was gospel. Bathe the boys three times a day? Sure. Isolate them from other children? She could do that. Move out of her house and buy another? You bet.

Yet in spite of all she did, Bowen couldn't shake a nagging sense of dread. Maybe this wasn't just an unlucky collection of symptoms, she thought. Maybe it was a rare disease.

In 1988, the year Evan was 2 and Michael was 1, both boys were put in intensive care with dangerously enlarged hearts. When Bowen asked the doctor to recommend a book on cardiomyopathy, the boys' condition, he replied, "You wouldn't understand the words. Why don't you concentrate on being a mother and I'll be the doctor?"

**When does an ordinary mother turn into a crusader?** Was it the day in 1990 that Evan was hospitalized once again with heart failure, and the doctor dismissed Shelley's request for a genetic consultation? This time, she cut him off. "I don't know if you heard me," Shelley said, her voice steely. "But if you're not going to do it, I'll find somebody who will." Something changed in that moment. She would not stand back again.

Bowen bought a stethoscope and kept it by her bedside; then she trained herself to listen to the boys' hearts for signs of trouble. On nights when they had colds or coughs, she rarely slept. Once, when Evan was congested and hacking, she crawled into bed next to him and drifted off with the stethoscope still in her ears, sleeping to the sound of her child's heartbeat.

By now, Bowen kept a suitcase filled with coloring books, paints and paintbrushes packed and ready near the door. At the hospital, the boys usually had their own room, with beds side by side. One day she came in and found them on the floor playing with the two little doll beds she had bought them. This had become their life, she thought, swallowing hard, and they didn't even find it odd.

In June, a packet of information arrived in the mail from the geneticist. The disease finally had a name: Barth syndrome, a rare genetic disorder that affects about one in 200,000 boys. The disease strikes three ways: with cardiomyopathy, low white-blood-cell count and general muscle weakness and fatigue. The boys' muscles, including the heart, had a cellular deficiency that made them too weak to produce energy. "Now I know what we're fighting," Shelley told Evan, who was hospitalized once again. "We can beat this!"

But there wasn't enough time. Moments later, when Bowen placed the tiny 5-year-old in a chair and turned to help change his bed linens, she heard him fall. Evan lay on the floor, unmoving.

As doctors pumped his heart, desperately trying to keep him alive, Shelley went into shock. Two days later, Evan was dead.

For weeks, Michael woke every morning, asking for his brother. Then, one day, he stopped asking. And for Shelley, deep in grief, that was hardest of all. He's forgetting the very best friend he ever had, she thought.

The geneticist's report had said that Barth syndrome was "lethal." Now Shelley knew that unless she did something, Michael was going to die, too. For the past two years, whenever doctors had used words she didn't understand, she had written them down and looked them up. She had learned that PVCs and PACs meant that Michael was having premature ventricular and atrial contractions—irregular heart rhythms. She learned the significance of T-waves on an electrocardiogram and how the QRS complex worked.

Now, she pored over medical books on rare diseases at the library. But she could find little on Barth syndrome, beyond the fact that it was described by a Dutch doctor named Peter G. Barth. When she plugged "Barth syndrome" into an Internet search engine, it came up blank.

By 1996, Michael's heart had deteriorated so much that his cardiologist suggested a transplant. Bowen realized that the doctor, like most American cardiologists, had never even seen a Barth syndrome child. Before they replaced Michael's heart, she wanted to talk to an expert who could address the entire constellation of symptoms, not just the heart.

"I'm calling Dr. Barth," she announced at home that night.

Her husband, Michael, a cautious, methodical man, was skeptical. "This is like finding out your child has polio," he observed later, "and deciding to call Jonas Salk on the phone." But he knew better than to stand in his wife's way once she had made up her mind.

Shelley got up when the 3:30 a.m. alarm rang; then she sat in her darkened house and dialed the Netherlands. Within minutes, Barth, a neurologist at Emma Children's Hospital in Amsterdam, was on the line.

"Fax me a list of questions," he said after listening to Bowen's story. "And bring Michael here to see me."

State medical assistance paid Michael's costs, and Bowen's Presbyterian church took up a collection to cover her plane ticket and expenses.

Finally, six weeks after her call to Dr. Barth, Bowen lugged two large file boxes aboard an airplane in Tampa. "Don't you want to check those?" asked the flight attendant.

"These are my children's medical records," Bowen replied, catching her breath. "If this plane goes down, I'll be swimming around trying to get them."

Michael was beside her on the plane, but this time, it was Bowen's heart that was racing. She had been on an airplane only two times in her life and was terrified of flying. And she wasn't even sure exactly where the Netherlands was.

research hospitals with clinics for children and next the American Academy of Pediatrics roster of cardiologists. Had they ever treated children with Barth syndrome?

Then one day in 1998, she went to the library and typed in "Barth syndrome" on the Internet for perhaps the hundredth time. This time, she found a query from a New Hampshire woman posted on a message board on a site for rare disorders of children. The woman had a 6-year-old son with Barth syndrome.

Bowen stared at the screen in disbelief. It doesn't have to be deadly, she thought. There's someone else. Within weeks, she had made contact with mothers of Barth boys in Nebraska, New Hampshire, Canada and Australia. She bought a computer and started a website, and within three

> Her husband was skeptical. "This is like finding out your child has polio and deciding to call Jonas Salk on the phone," he said.

**After eight years, 36 doctors, 47 hospital stays, and the loss of one child,** Shelley Bowen met Dr. Barth.

He was silver-haired, reserved—and curious to find out more about this persistent American woman. "How wonderful to finally meet you!" she cried, wrapping her arms around him. And then, "Help me."

After examining Michael, now 10, Barth told Bowen that if a boy survives the first five years, as Michael had, the prognosis improves dramatically. He suggested that Shelley hold off on a transplant because the heart conditions of Barth boys often improve over months and years. For the first time, Bowen felt a sense of hope.

Dr. Barth had a question of his own: Did Bowen know of other kids with the disease? When she said no, Barth and a colleague said there were others and urged her to find them.

Back home, sitting at a desk wedged into the hallway of her modest home behind a supermarket in Perry, Fla., she began a letter-writing campaign. First, she targeted

years she and her cyber-colleagues had organized the Barth Syndrome Foundation to help other families with Barth boys.

As for Michael, he's 16 now, a ninth-grader who makes straight A's in a study program combining high school classes, an online course and a tutor provided by the local school district. With his thick brown hair and freckles, he looks every bit a teenager. The only hint of health problems is his size: At five feet tall, he's small for his age.

Though Michael never had the transplant, he will be on heart medication for the rest of his life. And some activities will always be beyond his reach. Michael, like his mother, is an optimist. "I'm definitely going to college," he says emphatically. "I want to be a photographer or maybe go to veterinarian school."

His mom takes satisfaction in knowing there's a 39-year-old man in the Netherlands with Barth syndrome who has a job, a wife and family. And so Shelley Bowen smiles, thinking of her son, the boy who will become a man. ∎

# Charlie Would Have Loved THIS

## By J. P. McEvoy

In Hawaii on the vacation she had always dreamed about, something important was missing.

ILLUSTRATION BY ROSS MACDONALD

She was sitting beside me on the beach at Waikiki. Sounds romantic, doesn't it? But it wasn't really. There were many ladies just like her—tourists from everywhere—white haired, restless, lonely. On a small stage, flaming with tropical flowers, a colorful group of Hawaiian singers and dancers were broadcasting their weekly sun-kissed program of synthetic romance to the frostbitten unfortunates on the Mainland.

"This is your Isle of Golden Dreams, calling to you from across the sea," crooned the announcer. His assistant ran a few yards down to the lapping waves with a microphone.

"Listen, folks! The waves of Waikiki. Can't you see the surfboard riders? Can't you just picture those hula girls swaying under the palms?"

The white-haired lady beside me said, "Charlie would have loved this. It's just like we used to hear it on the radio back in Illinois. Saturday nights when Charlie came in from the fields, he'd turn on this program, 'Hawaii Calls,' and we'd listen, and Charlie would say, 'Mary, we're going there some day,' and I'd say, 'When?' and he'd say, 'Soon as we've saved up some money and get some time,' and I'd say, 'You've been saying that for years, Charlie, but every time we get a little money, you buy another 40 acres. Are you trying to buy up the whole state of Illinois?' That was a joke we had, and Charlie would laugh and say, 'No, I just want the piece next to me.' So Charlie never did get out here."

"You are listening to the Singing Surfriders," purred the announcer, "but unfortunately you cannot see the lovely Lani dancing her famous hula under the palms. She is wearing a green ti-leaf skirt and a red hibiscus in her long black hair."

The little white-haired lady said, "We had such good times together. If only Charlie was here with me now."

Every Sunday night, in the High Talking Chief's Long House on Waikiki Beach, Don the Beachcomber puts on a luau for the tourists. This is a Polynesian-type clambake where only the barbecued pig comes fully dressed, while the guests sit on the floor, kick off their shoes, drape leis of white gardenias or pink carnations around their necks, and the ladies stick a red hibiscus over their ear—the right ear if they have a man, the left if they want one.

Tourists milled around the bar, carrying bamboo tubes filled with rum concoctions playfully labeled Missionary Downfall, Cobra's Fang and the Vicious Virgin. I spotted my white-haired friend, timid and alone, but bravely sporting a man's aloha shirt that looked like an explosion in a paint factory. But the conventional black skirt and high-heeled shoes were definitely out of place in this technicolor jungle of muumuus, holokuus, sarongs, bare torsos and coconut hats.

I walked over and said, "Are you with anyone?"

"No," she said. "Is it all right to come alone?"

"You're not alone," I told her and hung a flower lei around her neck and kissed her cheek. "Let's go sit down. They're bringing in the barbecued pig."

I introduced her to my party, and they moved over to make room for her as she looked around a bit helplessly. "But everybody's sitting on the floor."

"That's right," I said. "Those creaking noises you hear are just old Mainland joints like yours and mine." She sat down on the floor beside me. "Now kick off your shoes and dive in," I told her.

Wooden platters were set before each guest but no knives or forks. My friend watched as we old-timers dug in with bare hands and licked our fingers. Then she followed suit, embarrassed at first, but quickly getting into the spirit of the occasion.

"What are we eating?" she asked. "Not that I care," she added quickly.

"This is pig baked underground with heated rocks. And this is laulau—butterfish wrapped in ti leaf. And this," I said, dipping it up with my fingers, "is the poi they sing about. It looks and tastes like paper hanger's paste. If you can scoop it up with one finger, it's one-finger poi. If you need two fingers, it's two-finger poi."

Don came over and tucked a red hibiscus into my friend's white hair over her right ear. I explained the difference, and she moved it to her left ear.

"Charlie would have loved this," she said.

And then the jungle drums started and a beautiful young Polynesian typhoon, wearing a crown of plumeria blossoms and a grass skirt, exploded into a dance.

> "Wouldn't it be wonderful if people could live like this all the time? Wear flowers in your hair and listen to music like this."

"Wouldn't it be wonderful if people could live like this all the time?" she said. "Kick off your shoes and sit on the floor and eat with your fingers and wear flowers in your hair and listen to music like that and watch dancers like what's-her-name there."

"Johnny," I said. "She comes from Pukapuka in the South Seas."

"Charlie always wanted to go there," she said. "There was a book, *White Shadows in the South Seas*. He used to read it aloud to me, and once we saw a movie by the same name, and he said, 'Someday I'll take you there.' But he kept putting it off. And when he died I wouldn't have been able to make this trip if it hadn't been for the insurance money he left."

A troupe from Samoa took the floor and did a dazzling fire dance. My friend sighed.

"I guess we waited too long." She shook her head a little, bewildered. "There's something wrong somewhere. What is the use of working yourself to death if you don't live to enjoy it?"

"Maybe we don't have to," I said. "When we want homes, we don't wait until we're too old to get them. We borrow the money and live in the houses while we pay it off. Lots of us do the same with cars. We don't walk our legs off until we need wheelchairs. We get the cars and manage somehow to pay for them. Suppose Charlie had added a few hundred more to the mortgage and brought you out here while you both could enjoy it. Wouldn't that have made a lot more sense than buying another 40 acres? Practical people would be a lot more practical if they were just a little more dreamy. Then they wouldn't put off living until they were dead. Someday we may even be practical enough to invest in our dreams first."

"Aloha!" cried Don the Beachcomber. "Let's sing the song we all know—

# "We waited too long. There's something wrong somewhere. What is the use of working yourself to death if you don't live to enjoy it?"

*One fond embrace*
*Before we now depart,*
*Until we meet again. ..."*

There's no sweeter, sadder song. Even in broad daylight you feel like crying like a baby when perfect strangers sing "Aloha" and wave farewell to you from Honolulu piers and airports. As the party ended we started out into the street in our bare feet.

The little white-haired lady from Illinois had forgotten her shoes under the table, but her red hibiscus dangled jauntily over her left ear, and there was a brave swing to the flower lei around her neck.

"You know what?" she said.

"Yes," I said. "Charlie would have loved this."

"That's for sure," she said, and she walked across the street to her lonely hotel room. ∎

## LAUGHTER, **THE BEST MEDICINE**

**THE CUSTOMER** only wanted half a head of lettuce and insisted the stock boy check with the manager before denying his request.

The boy approached his boss. "Some moron wants to buy half a head of lettuce," he said. Just then he saw that the customer was standing right behind him. "And this gentleman has kindly offered to buy the other half."

Later the manager said, "That was some pretty quick thinking. Tell me, where are you from, son?"

"Canada, sir," the boy replied.

"Really? And why did you leave?"

"Because there's nobody up there but tramps and hockey players."

"I see," said the manager. "You know, my wife is from Canada."

"Really?" said the boy. "What team does she play for?"

# A Troublesome BOY

He thought it would be fun to go away to school. Instead, the child who would become a great statesman found himself bewildered, making "little progress at my lessons and none at all at games."

I was on the whole considerably discouraged by my school days. All my contemporaries seemed in every way better adapted to the conditions of our little world. They were far better both at the games and at the lessons. It is not pleasant to feel oneself completely left behind at the very beginning of the race.

I was first threatened with school when I was 7 years old. At the time I was what grown-up people in their offhand way called "a troublesome boy." Although much that I had heard about school had made a disagreeable impression on my mind, an impression thoroughly borne out by the actual experience, I thought it would be fun to go away and live with so many other boys, and that we should have great adventures. Also I was told that "school days were the happiest time in one's life." All the boys enjoyed it. Some of my cousins

*By Winston S. Churchill*

had been quite sorry—I was told—to come home for the holidays. Cross-examined, the cousins did not confirm this; they only grinned.

It was a dark November afternoon when the last sound of my mother's departing carriage died away and I was taken into a Form room and told to sit at a desk. All the other boys were out of doors, and I was alone with the Form Master. He produced a thin, greeny-brown-covered book.

"This is a Latin grammar." He opened it at a well-thumbed page. "You must learn this," he said, pointing to several words in a frame of lines. "I will come back in half an hour and see what you know."

Behold me then on a gloomy evening, with an aching heart, seated in front of the declension of *mensa*.

What on earth did it mean? It seemed absolute rigmarole to me. However, there was one thing I could always do: I could learn by heart.

In due course the Master returned.

"Have you learned it?" he asked.

"I think I can say it, sir," I replied; and I grabbed it off.

He seemed so satisfied with this that I was emboldened to ask a question.

"What does it mean, sir?"

"It means what it says. *Mensa*, a table."

"Then why does *mensa* also mean O table," I inquired, "and what does O table mean?"

"*Mensa*, O table, is the vocative case," he replied. "You would use that in speaking to a table."

"But I never do," I blurted out in honest amazement.

Such was my first introduction to the classics from which, I have been told, many of our cleverest men have derived so much solace and profit.

Flogging with the birch was a great feature in the curriculum. Two or three times a month the whole school was marshaled in the Library, and one or more delinquents were haled off to an adjoining apartment and there flogged until they bled freely, while the rest sat quaking, listening to their screams. How I hated this school, and what a life of anxiety I lived there for more than two years! I made very little progress at my lessons and none at all at games. The greatest pleasure I had was reading. When I was nine and a half my father gave me *Treasure Island*, and I remember the delight with which I devoured it. My teachers saw me at once backward and precocious, reading books beyond my years and yet at the bottom of the Form. They were offended. They had large resources of compulsion at their disposal, but I was stubborn.

Where my reason, imagination or interest was not engaged, I would not or I could not learn. In all the 12 years I was at school no one ever succeeded in making me write a Latin verse or learn any Greek except the alphabet. To stimulate my flagging interest they told me that Mr. Gladstone read Homer for fun, which I thought served him right.

I had scarcely passed my twelfth birthday when I entered the inhospitable regions of examinations. These were a great trial to me. The subjects which were dearest to the examiners were almost invariably those I fancied least. I would have liked to have been examined in history, poetry and writing essays. The examiners, on the other hand, were partial to Latin and mathematics. Moreover, I should have liked to be asked to say what I knew. They always tried to ask what I did not know. When I would have willingly displayed my knowledge, they sought to expose my ignorance. This sort of treatment had only one result: I did not do well in examinations.

This was especially true of my entrance examination to Harrow. The Headmaster, Dr. Welldon, however, took a broad-minded view of my Latin prose; he showed discernment in judging my general ability. This was remarkable because I was found unable to answer a single question in the Latin paper. I wrote my name at the top of the page. I wrote down the number of the question: I. After much reflection I put a bracket round it thus: (I). But thereafter I could not think of anything connected with it that was either relevant or true. Incidentally there arrived from nowhere in particular a blot and several smudges. I gazed for two whole hours at this sad spectacle, and then merciful ushers collected my piece of foolscap. It was from these slender indications of scholarship that Dr. Welldon drew the conclusion that I was worthy to pass into Harrow. It is very much to his credit. It showed that he was a man capable of looking beneath the surface of things, a man not dependent upon paper manifestations. I have always had the greatest regard for him.

On exams, Churchill wanted "to be asked to say what I knew. They always tried to ask what I did not know." The result? "I did not do well."

I was in due course placed in the lowest division of the bottom Form. I continued in this unpretentious situation for nearly a year. However, by being so long in the lowest Form I gained an immense advantage over the cleverer boys. They all went on to learn Latin and Greek and splendid things like that. But I was taught English. We were considered such dunces that we could learn only English. As I remained in the Third Fourth three times as long as anyone else, I had three times as much of it. I learned it thoroughly. Thus I got into my bones the essential structure of the ordinary British sentence—which is a noble thing. And when in after years my schoolfellows who had won prizes and distinction for writing such beautiful Latin poetry and pithy Greek epigrams had to come down again to common English to earn their living or make their way, I did not feel myself at any disadvantage.

It was thought incongruous that, while I apparently stagnated in the lowest Form, I should gain a prize open to the whole school for reciting to the Headmaster 1,200 lines of Macaulay's "Lays of Ancient Rome" without making a single mistake. I also succeeded in passing the preliminary examination for the Army while many boys far above me failed in it. I also had a piece of good luck. We knew that among other questions we should be asked to draw from memory a map of some country or other. The night before, by way of final preparation, I put the names of all the maps in the atlas into a hat and drew out New Zealand. I applied my good memory to the geography of that Dominion. Sure enough the first question in the paper was: "Draw a map of New Zealand." Henceforward all my education was directed in the Army class to passing into Sandhurst. Officially I never got out of the Lower School at Harrow.

It took me three tries to pass into Sandhurst. There were five subjects of which Mathematics, Latin and English were obligatory, and I chose in addition French and Chemistry. In this hand I held only a pair of Kings—English and Chemistry. Nothing less than three would open the jackpot. I had to find another useful card. Latin I could not learn. French was interesting but rather tricky. So there remained only mathematics. I turned to them—I turned on them—in desperation.

Of course what I call Mathematics is only what the Civil Service Commissioners expected you to know to pass a very rudimentary examination. Nevertheless, when I plunged in I was soon out of my depth. I was soon in a strange corridor of things called Sines, Cosines and Tangents. Apparently they were very important, especially when multiplied by each other or by themselves! They had also this merit—you could learn many of their evolutions off by heart. There was a question in my third and last examination about these Cosines and Tangents in a highly square-rooted condition which must have been decisive upon the whole of my after life. But luckily I had seen its ugly face only a few days before and recognized it at first sight.

I have never met any of these creatures since. With my third and successful examination they passed away like the phantasmagoria of a fevered dream. I am assured that they are most helpful in engineering, astronomy and things like that. I am glad there are quite a number of people born with a gift and a liking for all of this; like great chess players, for example, who play 16 games at once blindfold and die quite soon of epilepsy.

> He decided that "my school years form the only unhappy period of my life. I would far rather have been apprenticed as a bricklayer's mate."

The practical point is that, if I had not been asked this particular question about these Cosines or Tangents, I might have gone into the Church and preached orthodox sermons in a spirit of audacious contradiction to the age. I might have gone into the City and made a fortune. I might even have gravitated to the Bar, and persons might have been hanged through my defense who now nurse their guilty secrets with complacency.

In retrospect my school years form the only barren and unhappy period of my life. Actually, no doubt, they were buoyed up by the laughter and high spirits of youth. But I would far rather have been apprenticed as a bricklayer's mate or run errands as a messenger boy. It would have been real; it would have been natural; it would have taught me more; and I should have done it much better.

I am all for the Public Schools, but I do not want to go there again. ■

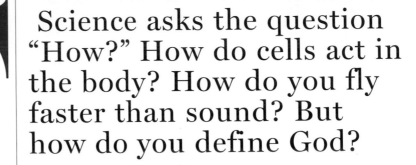

Science asks the question "How?" How do cells act in the body? How do you fly faster than sound? But how do you define God?

# Can a Scientist Believe in GOD?

*By Warren Weaver*

Science and religion. Science is the activity whereby man attempts to gain understanding and control of nature. I don't feel the need to qualify this statement by saying, "This is my kind of science or this is what science means to me."

ILLUSTRATION BY NICK DEWAR

Religion, on the other hand, is a highly personal affair. I can tell you only what it means to me: first, a guide to conduct; second, the theory of the moral meaning of our existence.

Science tries to answer the question "How?" How do cells act in the body? How do you design an airplane that will fly faster than sound? Religion, by contrast, tries to answer the question "Why?" Why was man created? Why ought I to tell the truth?

Science attempts to analyze how things and people and animals behave; it has no concern whether this behavior is good or bad. Religion is precisely the quest for such answers.

How do you define God? When I am troubled or afraid or deeply concerned for those I love, when I listen to the hymns that go back to the loveliest memories of my childhood, then God is to me an emotional and comforting God—a protecting Father.

> It gratifies me that I am able to think about God in ways intellectually satisfying and consistent with the thinking I try to do along scientific lines.

When I am trying to work out a problem of right and wrong, then God is a clear and unambiguous voice, an unfailing source of moral guidance. I do not understand how these things happen; but I know perfectly well, if I listen to this voice, what is the right thing to do. I have many times been uncertain as to what course of action would best serve a certain practical purpose; but I cannot think of a single instance in my life when I asked what was the really *right* thing to do and the answer was not forthcoming.

These two statements cover my everyday relationship with God. I do not find it necessary to try to analyze them in logical terms. They state facts of experience. You can no more convince me that there is no such God than you can convince me that a table or a rock is not solid—in each case the evidence is simple, direct and uniform.

As a scientist familiar with detailed explanations of the atomic structure of, say, the table and the rock, it does not disturb me that these everyday concepts of God do not offer me a detailed logical explanation. God on an intellectual plane (corresponding to the theoretical plane of the physicist) is something else, and just as a scientist would expect, abstract. And it gratifies me that, in addition to the everyday way, I am able to think about God in ways intellectually satisfying and consistent with the thinking I try to do along scientific lines.

God is, to me, the name behind a consistent set of phenomena, which are all recognizable in terms of moral purpose and which deal with the control of man's destiny.

Can a scientist believe in God? Scientists are precisely the persons who believe in the unseeable, the essentially undefinable. No scientist has ever *seen* an electron. "Electron" is simply the name for a consistent set of things that happen in certain circumstances. Yet nothing is more "real" to a scientist than an electron. Chairs, tables, rocks—these are not very "real" to him, if he thinks deeply. A table, viewed with the precise tools of the atomic physicist, is a shadowy, swirling set of electronic charges, in themselves vague and elusive. So viewed, the table completely loses its large-scale illusion of solidity.

The scientist is the last to expect that an "ultimate explanation" is going to solve familiar ideas. He is just the one who should not say that an abstract concept of God results in an "unreal" God. To him, the real is what is *universally experienced*. He raises a basic question: "Does the definition *work* successfully?" "Electron" is only the name behind a set of phenomena, but essentially all physicists agree as to what these electron phenomena are. If there is this kind of consistency, then a definition "works"— and the scientist finds it acceptable and satisfying. Man has not attained the same agreement for what can be called God phenomena, yet I accept the abstract and intellectual idea of God for three reasons:

First, in the total history of man, there has been an impressive amount of general agreement about the existence of "God." This agreement is not so logically precise as the agreements about electrons; but far, far more people believe and have believed in God than believe or have ever believed in electrons.

Second, I know I cannot think through the realm of religious experience as satisfactorily as I can through less important problems. But the nuclear physicist today has only incomplete and contradictory theories. Yet the theories work pretty well and represent the best knowledge we have on the subject.

Third, I accept the two sets of ideas of God—the everyday concept of an emotional and intuitive God, and the intellectual concept of an abstract God—for the very good reason that I find both of them personally satisfying. It does not at all worry me that these are two rather different sets of ideas. Scientists think an electron can be two wholly inconsistent things; it is a little narrow to expect so much less of God.

Can a scientist believe the Bible? I think that God has revealed Himself to many at many times and in many places. Indeed, He continuously reveals Himself to man today: Every new discovery of science is further "revelation" of the order God built into His universe.

I believe that the Bible is the purest revelation we have of the nature and goodness of God. It seems to me inevitable that the human record of divine truth should exhibit a little human frailty along with much divine truth. It seems to me quite unnecessary to be disturbed over minor eccentricities in the record. The reports of miraculous happenings are to me understandable as poetic exaggeration or as ancient interpretations of events that we would not consider miraculous today. ■

# LAUGHTER, **THE BEST MEDICINE**

**RANDY THE DISHWASHER REPAIRMAN** was given specific instructions concerning the woman's two pets. "The Rottweiler won't hurt you, even though it looks fierce, but whatever you do, don't talk to the parrot."

Randy let himself in and set to work, and the dog just lay quietly on the carpet. But the parrot mocked him mercilessly the whole time. "Wow, you're pretty fat," the bird would say. "Hey, fatso, you couldn't change the batteries in a flashlight, let alone fix a dishwasher."

Before long, Randy had had enough. "You know, bird, you think you're pretty smart for someone with a brain the size of a pea."

The parrot was silent for a moment and then, with a gleam in its eye, said, "All right. Get him, Spike."

**MILES AND MARGARET** had been arguing, and finally they stopped speaking to each other altogether. On Sunday night Miles remembered that he had an important meeting the next morning. Not wanting to be the first to break the silence, he wrote a note asking Margaret if she would wake him at 5:00.

The next day he awoke to see that it was 9:00. Furious, he leapt out of bed and spotted a note on the nightstand:

"It's 5:00. Time to get up!"

**A GUY** shows up late for work. The boss yells, "You should've been here at 8:30!"

The guy replies, "Why? What happened at 8:30?"

**THE POLICE OFFICER** pulled over a guy driving a convertible because he had a penguin riding in the passenger seat.

"Hey, buddy, is that an actual penguin?"

"Yeah. I just picked him up."

"Well, why don't you take him to the zoo?"

The guy agreed, but the very next day the cop saw him drive by again with the penguin sitting beside him.

"I thought I told you to take that thing to the zoo," said the officer.

"I did," the guy replied. "And we had such a good time, tonight we're going to a hockey game."

**WHEN THE PATROLMAN** saw the man speed past, he pulled him over and asked for his license and registration.

"I lost my license after my fifth DWI," the guy replied calmly. "I'll give you the registration, but don't freak out when I open the glove box because I've got a couple of guns in there. And if you search the car, don't be surprised if you find some drugs in the trunk."

Alarmed, the cop called for backup. Moments later a SWAT team swept down on the car. The driver was handcuffed as the team searched the vehicle.

"There's no drugs or guns in this car, buddy," the SWAT leader said to the driver.

"Of course not," the man replied. "And I suppose that cop told you I was speeding, too."

Bullet, the golden retriever they'd saved from death, immediately bonded with Troy and Pam Sica's baby. And that was the beginning of a truly remarkable story.

# Sixth Sense

## By Chris Bohjalian

When Hollywood is looking for the next wonder dog, they probably won't cast Bullet of Bellport, Long Island. Bullet is a 15-year-old golden retriever whose snout has gone grizzled with age and who moves with the grace and agility of a box turtle waddling across a highway. He has a weak heart and tumors. Even owners who truly love their pets probably would have euthanized Bullet some time ago.

Fortunately, Bullet is owned by Pam Sica, a woman who understands the meaning of friendship and the importance of faith.

Pam and her husband, Troy Sica, live in a modest but immaculately well-maintained single-story home with chestnut brown shingles and a front walkway bordered by manicured evergreen trees and shrubs. The house is in a quiet residential neighborhood not far from the Great South Bay separating Long Island from Fire Island. Pam is a bartender at an upscale hotel, and Troy is an air traffic controller.

**In April of 2000, Pam learned that her beloved Bullet** had a tumor the size of a pea on his liver. Given the dog's age, Dr. Laurence Cangro recommended that they merely monitor the growth.

Pam was devastated. She had lost other pets, but she had built a special bond with Bullet. He had come into her life as a seven-week-old puppy in a gift basket on her front porch with a red bow around him and a card that asked, "Will you be my Mommy?"

For over a decade the dog had, in many ways, been her baby. Pam and Troy had tried to conceive a child for several years, and though she'd become pregnant four times, each pregnancy ended in a miscarriage. "My whole life was my animals because they said I could never have children," Pam says. She was 41 the year she got the bad news about Bullet.

By August the tumor had mushroomed, and Dr. Cangro realized that the Sicas faced some hard choices. "The concern with liver masses is that they can tear and bleed. There was a big risk of hemorrhaging to death if it ruptured," Cangro recalls. But surgery on a golden retriever this old would be hazardous—and also cost thousands of dollars.

"In my experience, maybe one in ten people would go to that extent and that expense for a dog that old," Cangro says.

But Pam and Troy were ready to do just that—even if it meant financial hardship. Indeed, the couple would ultimately spend close to $5,000 on tests, surgery and postoperative care. "My friends and family said I was crazy spending that kind of money," Pam recalls. "But Bullet gave me my best years as my friend. How could I not do this for him?"

Troy and Pam took the dog to their local priest to have him blessed, and on September 1, 2000, a heart specialist and a veterinary surgeon removed the tumor from Bullet's liver.

Not only did Bullet survive the surgery, he surprised the vets by waking up hungry from anesthesia. He was home with the Sicas within days.

It was a little miracle, and then about a year later another happened. While vacationing at Walt Disney World, of all places, Pam took a home pregnancy test that turned out positive.

Quite sure that this would be her last chance, Pam did everything that she could to keep this baby. She steadily decreased the days she worked throughout the fall and winter until she was down to two evenings a week. Then, following her doctor's instructions, she stopped working completely early in the third trimester.

**Troy Joseph Sica was born at 11:32 a.m. on April 10,** 2002—eyes the color of antique blue moonstones and a thick swatch of nutmeg-brown hair. Even before Pam brought baby Troy home, she prepared Bullet for the new arrival. She had her husband bring the dog the baby blanket that the infant had been swaddled in at the hospital so he would grow comfortable with the new scent.

That first evening, Bullet retrieved the blanket from the den, and dragged it to the pair of cushy dog beds in which he sleeps in the kitchen. And any lingering fears Pam had

> # Suddenly, Bullet was behind Pam, barking, hopping and jumping two and three inches off the floor. Then he started leading her down the hallway.

that Bullet might become jealous of the baby were quickly dispelled when they brought him into the house.

"The baby and the dog bonded right away," Pam says. "When the baby cried, Bullet would pick up his head to make sure that Troy or I were taking care of him."

**Around five o'clock in the morning on May 1,** two weeks after he came home, baby Troy was dozing on his back on the bed in the couple's bedroom, surrounded by pillows. His dad was in the shower getting ready to go to work, and Pam was in the kitchen warming up a bottle.

Suddenly Bullet was behind her in the kitchen doorway—barking and hopping and jumping two and three inches off the floor. "And then," Pam vividly recalls, "he started trying to lead me down the hallway to the bedroom."

At first Pam thought that Bullet had been incontinent and was trying to inform her that he'd had an accident in the bedroom. No hurry. She didn't follow him immediately. She made a detour to the bathroom to ask Troy to double-check the temperature of the bottle. But Bullet grew even more frantic in his efforts to coax her down the hall—jumping with increasing frenzy and more energy than she had seen in years.

Finally she followed him, moving with the tired gait of a new mother at five in the morning.

When she came to the bedroom door she gasped and dropped the bottle she was carrying. There on the bed was little Troy, just where she'd left him—but his skin had turned an almost neon shade of blue. His body grew limp and a desperate gurgle emanated from his throat as he struggled to breathe.

She pulled the infant from the bed. "Please, God, don't take my baby!" she cried, and she raced into the bathroom where her husband was finishing his shower.

While Troy flipped the child onto his stomach and started patting his back, trying to dislodge whatever was blocking his windpipe, Pam called 911.

A code Delta alert—the highest level respiratory emergency—went out. Within minutes police were on the scene. And in a stroke of good fortune, Damon Alberts, an advanced emergency medical technician, lived just around the corner from the Sicas. He and the rest of his crew from the South Country Ambulance Company arrived at the house shortly thereafter.

The EMTs administered high-concentration oxygen to the infant, blowing the air in front of baby Troy's mouth and nose because his head was too small for the mask. Within a minute the blue began to recede from his face, and his color returned to normal. He was breathing again on his own. But he was not out of danger.

The EMTs rushed him by ambulance to Brookhaven Memorial Hospital Medical Center. There he stopped breathing once more and had to be resuscitated again.

Later that morning he was transferred to Stony Brook University Hospital's pediatric ICU, where he was diagnosed with pneumonia. He spent four days on a ventilator and received two weeks of IV antibiotics to help him fight off the infection.

"He's going to lead a normal, healthy life, as long as he wears his seatbelt and doesn't drink and drive," says Dr. Thomas Biancaniello, the director of pediatric cardiology at Stony Brook, with a smile.

Had Bullet not insisted that Pam drop what she was doing and follow him into the bedroom, however, it might have been otherwise. Dr. Marc Salzberg, the chief medical officer of Brookhaven Hospital, says, "Pneumonia is more dangerous in a newborn. Their brains are more vulnerable to oxygen deprivation, since the human brain isn't fully developed until age two. Deprived of oxygen for more than a few minutes, a newborn will have brain damage or die."

But how did Bullet know the baby was in trouble?

"Dogs are keen observers of body language," explains Dr. Marty Becker, a veterinarian and writer. "They spend hour upon hour studying our every movement, listening to the cadence of our breathing, the very beat of our hearts. I can see [that] dog watch the absence of movement, fail to hear

> When something is wrong, the veterinarian explained, dogs "go to the leader of the pack for guidance or help. The leader of Bullet's pack is Pam."

a breath and know something was wrong. When something is wrong, they immediately go to the leader of the pack for guidance or help. In this case, the leader of Bullet's pack is Pam."

And so perhaps the real miracle of this story isn't Bullet's comprehension that his new pack mate on the bed was in serious trouble. Rather, the real wonder might be Pam's faith two years ago that her elderly dog still had a few good years left in him.

"I gave Bullet life, and he gave me a life back," she says. ■

## HUMOR IN UNIFORM

**MY FATHER,** a retired Air Force pilot, often sprinkles his conversation with aviation jargon. I didn't realize what flying had meant to him, however, until the day he showed me the folder with his last will and testament. It was labeled "Cleared for departure."

-CHERYL E. DRAKE

# Your SECOND JOB

By Dr. Albert Schweitzer

The esteemed Nobel Peace Prize winner explains the obligation we all have to help others.

Often people say, "I would like to do some good in the world. But with so many responsibilities at home and in business, my nose is always to the grindstone. I am sunk in my own petty affairs, and there is no chance for my life to mean anything."

This is a common and dangerous error. In helpfulness to others, every man can find on his own doorstep adventures for the soul—our surest satisfaction. To know this happiness, one does not have to neglect duties or do spectacular things.

This career for the spirit I call "your second job." In this there is no pay except the privilege of doing it. In it you will encounter noble

chances and find deep strength. Here all your reserve power can be put to work, for what the world lacks most today is men who occupy themselves with the needs of other men. In this unselfish labor a blessing falls on both the helper and the helped.

Without such spiritual adventures the man or woman of today walks in darkness. In the pressures of modern society we tend to lose our individuality. Our craving for creation and self-expression is stifled; true civilization is to that extent retarded.

What is the remedy? No matter how busy one is, any human being can assert his personality by seizing every opportunity for spiritual activity. How? By his second job: by means of personal action, on however small a scale, for the good of his fellow men.

He will not have to look far for opportunities. Our greatest mistake, as individuals, is that we walk through our life with closed eyes and do not notice our chances. As soon as we open our eyes and deliberately search we see many who need help, not in big things but in the littlest things. Wherever a man turns he can find someone who needs him.

One day I was traveling through Germany in a third-class railway carriage beside an eager youth who sat as if looking

his own commission. Soldiers from out-of-town camps were being allowed leave in the city before going to the front. So at eight o'clock the old cabby appeared at a railroad station and looked for puzzled troopers. Four or five times every night, right up to demobilization, he served as a volunteer guide through the maze of London streets.

From a feeling of embarrassment, we hesitate to approach a stranger. The fear of being repulsed is the cause of a great deal of coldness in the world; when we seem indifferent we are often merely timid. The adventurous soul must break that barrier, resolving in advance not to mind a rebuff. If we dare with wisdom, always maintaining a certain reserve in our approach, we find that when we open ourselves we open doors in others.

Especially in great cities do the doors of the heart need to be opened. Love is always lonely in crowds. Country and village people know each other and realize some common dependence, but the inhabitants of cities are strangers who pass without salute—so isolated, so separate, often so lost and despairing. What a stupendous opportunity is waiting there for men and women who are willing to be simply human!

Begin anywhere—in office, factory, subway. There may have been smiles across a streetcar aisle that stayed the purpose of suicide. Often a friendly glance is like a single ray of sunshine, piercing a darkness we ourselves may not dream is there.

> "My only son is in the hospital, very ill. But I am afraid I shall get lost in the city."

As I look back upon my youth I realize how important to me were the help, understanding and courage, the gentleness and wisdom so many people gave me. These men and women entered into my life and became powers within me. But they never knew it. Nor did I perceive the real significance of their help at the time.

We all owe so much to others; and we may well ask ourselves, what will others owe to *us*? The complete answer must remain hidden from us, although we are often allowed to see some little fraction of it so that we may not lose courage. You may be sure, however, that the effect of your own life on those around you is—or can be—great indeed.

for something unseen. Facing him was a fretful and plainly worried old man. Presently the lad remarked that it would be dark before we reached the nearest large city.

"I don't know what I shall do when we get there," said the old man anxiously. "My only son is in the hospital, very ill. I had a telegram to come at once. I must see him before he dies. But I am from the country, and I'm afraid I shall get lost in the city."

To which the young man replied, "I know the city well. I will get off with you and take you to your son. Then I will catch a later train."

As they left the compartment they walked together like brothers.

Who can assay the effect of that small kind deed? You, too, can watch for the little things that need to be done.

During the First World War a cockney cab driver was declared too old for military service. From one bureau to another he went, offering to make himself useful in spare time and always being turned away. Finally he gave himself

Whatever you have received more than others—in health, in talents, in ability, in success, in a pleasant childhood, in harmonious conditions of home life—all this you must not take to yourself as a matter of course. In gratitude for your good fortune, you must render in return some sacrifice of your own life for other life.

For those who have suffered in special ways there are special opportunities. For example, there is the fellowship of those who bear the mark of pain. If you have been delivered from bodily anguish, you must not think you are free. From that moment on, you feel bound to help to bring others to deliverance. If an operation has saved you from death or torture, do your part to make it possible for medical science to reach some other place where death and agony still rule unhindered. So with the mother whose child has been saved, and the children whose father's last torment was made tolerable by a doctor's skill; all must join in seeing to it that others may know those blessings also.

In renunciation and sacrifice we must give, most of all, of ourselves. To hand ten dollars to someone who needs it is not a sacrifice if you can well afford the money. The widow's mite was worth more than all the rich men's donations because her mite was her all. In our own ways we must give something that it is a wrench to part with, if it is only time from the cinema, from favorite games or from our other pleasures.

I hear people say, "Oh, if I were only rich, I would do great things to help people." But we all *can* be rich in love and generosity. Moreover, if we give with care, if we find out the exact wants of those who need our help most, we are giving our own worth more than all the money in the world.

And by some working of the universal law, as you give of love, you are given more love and happiness to go on with!

Organized welfare work is, of course, necessary; but the gaps in it must be filled by personal service, performed with loving-kindness. A charitable organization is a complex affair; like an automobile, it needs a broad highway to run on. It cannot penetrate the little bypaths; those are for men and women to walk through, with open eyes full of comprehension.

We cannot abdicate our conscience to an organization, nor to a government. "Am I my brother's keeper?" Most certainly I am! I cannot escape my responsibility by saying the State will do all that is necessary. It is a tragedy that nowadays so many think and feel otherwise.

Even in family life, children are coming to believe they do not have to take care of the old folks. But old-age pensions do not relieve children of their duties. To dehumanize such care is wrong because it abolishes the principle of love, which is the foundation in upbuilding human beings and civilization itself.

Tenderness toward those weaker than ourselves strengthens the heart toward life itself. We do terrible things to one another because we do not have comprehension and pity. The moment we understand and feel sorry for the next man and forgive him, we wash ourselves, and it is a cleaner world.

But why must I forgive my fellow man?

Because, if I do not forgive everyone, I shall be untrue to myself. I shall then be acting as if I were innocent of the same offenses, and I am not. I must forgive lies directed against me because so many times my own conduct has been blotted by lies. I must forgive the lovelessness, the hatred, the slander, the fraud, the arrogance that I encounter, since I myself have so often lacked love and have hated, slandered, defrauded

and been arrogant. And I must forgive without noise or fuss. In general, I do not succeed in forgiving fully; I do not even get as far as being always just. But he who tries to live by this principle, simple and hard as it is, will know the real adventures and triumphs of the soul.

A man has done us a wrong. Are we to wait for him to ask our forgiveness? No! He may never ask pardon, and then we shall never forgive, which is evil. No, let us say, instead, "It does not exist!"

In a railway station I watch a man with dustpan and broom sweeping up refuse in the waiting room. He cleans a portion, then moves on to the next. But let him look back

> # The fear of being repulsed is the cause of a great deal of coldness in the world; when we seem to be indifferent, we are often merely timid.

over his shoulder and he will behold a man throwing a cigar stump on the floor, a child scattering paper around— more litter accumulating where a moment before he had it all swept clean. Yet he has to go right on with his work and feel no rage. So must we all! In my personal relations with people I must never be without my pan and broom. I must continually clean up the litter. I must rid myself of dead and useless things. If the leaves do not drop off the trees in autumn, there will be no room for new leaves in the spring.

You may think it is a wonderful life my wife and I have in the equatorial jungle. That is merely where we happen to be. But you can have a still more wonderful life by staying where you happen to be, putting your soul to the test in a thousand little trials and winning triumphs of love.

Such a career of the spirit demands patience, devotion, daring. It calls for strength of will and the determination to love: the greatest test of a man. But in this hard "second job" is to be found the only true happiness. ∎

*As told to Fulton Oursler*

# Credits

All the stories in [Reader's Digest True Lives] previously appeared in *Reader's Digest* magazine. We would like to thank the following contributors and publishers for permission to reprint material.